"This re-examination of the work of Robert Stoller in the light of contemporary thinking offers psychoanalysts a unique and thoughtful perspective, free from the rhetoric and ideology of political correctness and culture wars on gender, core gender identity, sexual excitement, sexual fantasy and the erotic lives of humans."
Howard B. Levine, *Editor-in-Chief of The Routledge W.R. Bion Studies Series*

"In an era of 'toxic masculinity' and attacks on the 'feminine,' this unique book delivers important understandings to clinical practitioners and analytically-oriented social theorists alike."
Michael J. Diamond, Ph.D, *Training and Supervising Analyst, Los Angeles Institute and Society for Psychoanalytic Studies*

"This thoughtful and long overdue study of Stoller's work provides insight into the role that fantasy, fetishization, and arousal play in the development of the male psyche."
Gilbert Herdt, Ph.D, *anthropologist and author of Third Sex, Third Gender*

Perversity, Pornography, and the Psychology of the Male Species

This book presents an overview of present-day psychoanalytic thinking about the perverse spectrum—perversions proper, perverse forms of thinking (disavowing reality) and of relating (manipulating others for one's own gain at the other's expense), and perverse character structure (toying with another's sense of what's real)—culminating in a clinical exploration of the challenges associated with treating patients who manifest perverse transference reactions.

Robert Stoller's theories about sexual fantasy, perversity, and the development of gender identity constitute a model of male psychological development that contradicts Freud's belief about the advantages of being born male. When a boy realizes his body differs from that of his mother, noted Stoller, the boy ceases to feel as close to her as he had once felt, which is a calamity the boy must bear and mourn. The boy's burgeoning sense of superiority, associated with the phallic narcissistic stage of development, helps counter the loss. Fixation at this stage is not the norm as Stoller had imagined; rather, it helps account for what is colloquially referred to as "toxic masculinity." The task of individuating from mother colors a man's subsequent relationships with women, beginning with the boy's efforts to break free of his mother followed by a subsequent struggle against the urge to be reunited with the primal mother, which contributes to men's dread of women. Rereading Stoller clarifies the role objectification/fetishization, sexualization, and perversity play in the lives of men—the extent to which male fantasy is tinged with hostility. It also challenges our thinking about gender and gender identity.

With fascinating clinical vignettes and a deep understanding of the source material, this is key reading for psychoanalysts and psychotherapists working with men.

Richard Tuch is a Volunteer Clinical Professor of Psychiatry at the David Geffen School of Medicine, University of California, Los Angeles. He is a Training and Supervising Analyst at The New Center for Psychoanalysis (Los Angeles) and the Psychoanalytic Center of California (Los Angeles). His interest in the work of Robert Stoller is directly related to personal experiences he had being taught by Professor Stoller when he was in psychiatric training at UCLA.

Perversity, Pornography, and the Psychology of the Male Species

An Overdue Rethinking of Robert Stoller's Gender Theories

Richard Tuch

Routledge
Taylor & Francis Group

LONDON AND NEW YORK

Designed cover image: Getty Image © Klaus Vedfelt

First published 2026
by Routledge
4 Park Square, Milton Park, Abingdon, Oxon OX14 4RN

and by Routledge
605 Third Avenue, New York, NY 10158

Routledge is an imprint of the Taylor & Francis Group, an informa business

British Library Cataloguing-in-Publication Data
A catalogue record for this book is available from the British Library

ISBN: 978-1-032-97475-0 (hbk)
ISBN: 978-1-041-00448-6 (pbk)
ISBN: 978-1-003-60933-9 (ebk)

DOI: 10.4324/9781003609339

Typeset in Optima
by Taylor & Francis Books

To my wife, Sunnye—my life mate and lifeboat.
To my children, Alex, Zachary, and Maguy Michelman-Tuch.
To my patients and students, from whom I learn much.
And to Robert Stoller, who inspired me and taught me how to write.

Contents

An Introduction

One of my chief aims in writing this book was to provide readers with a much overdue rethinking of Stoller's original theories. Seeing that this year (2025) marks the 50th anniversary of the publication of Stoller's provocatively entitled book *Perversion: The Erotic Form of Hatred*, the time seemed ripe for just such a project. The book not only explores perversion from Stoller's perspective, but it also traces how psychoanalytic thinking about perversion has evolved over time, reviewing the works of such authors as Milton Glasser, Janine Chasseguet-Smirgel, Masud Khan, Jacob Arlow, Phyllis Greenacre, and Jacque Lacan.

Some strongly object to using the term "perversion" given that the term had been used pejoratively to pathologize perfectly normal behaviors—men loving men or sadists and masochists engaged in consensual sex play that suits their mutual needs. The negative connotation of "perversion" and "perversity" led some to completely erase these terms from their vocabulary. Stoller insisted on using the term "perversion"—despite its negative connotation—seeing that no other single term adequately captured the panoply of elements that coalesced into a recognizable and repetitive core complex of behaviors, thoughts, feelings, fantasies, and attitudes.

Stoller took care to differentiate variations from the norm—such as homosexuality, which he viewed as nonpathological—from the sorts of fantasies, fantasy-based behaviors and ways of thinking he deemed "perverse."[1] He insisted that "perversion" not be used to refer to the "whom" with whom one is "doing it," nor what it is that one is doing when one is "doing it." Rather, he reserved the term to define a set of sexual fantasies and practices that are imbued with specific sorts of meanings, which makes the meaning of such fantasies the essence of what constitutes perversion and perversity. Stoller referred to such fantasies as erotic plots or sexual daydreams—akin to Laufer's (1976, 1981, 1989) "central masturbatory fantasy."

Stoller was fascinated with individuals whose way of living was out of keeping with how the "average" man (and woman) lived. Much in the same way that Diane Arbus (1923–1971) captured the photographic images of marginalized groups of people to humanize them for viewers who might otherwise have considered them "freaks,"[2] Stoller was comparably drawn to unusual people who had a tale to tale about the lives they were living. He was amongst the earliest psychiatrists to take a serious interest in people who felt at odds with their bodies (transsexuals) and he was at the forefront of the movement that succeeded at talking the American Psychiatric Association into de-pathologizing homosexuality by getting that "diagnosis" removed from the Diagnostic and Statistical Manual (DSM) in 1973, arguing homosexuality was "part of the natural realm" (Stoller 1973, p. 1207). He was fascinated by individuals whose sexual fantasies pictured them being mistreated, repeating painful and shameful childhood experiences, and he took an active interest in studying the storylines of scripted pornographic films, which led him to realize the extent to which sadistic impulses were expressed in the porn men love to watch. His source material didn't so much come from the couch as it came from interviews he conducted with professionals working in the porn industry, the world capital of which was located in the San Fernando Valley, situated just over the hill from his on-campus office at the University of California in West Los Angeles.

Stoller (1973) was convinced that most, perhaps all male fantasies and men's preferred fantasy-based pornography is perverse, which many readers will likely consider a stretch. He raised the question: "Whether there is such a thing as 'non-perverse sexuality' in men..." (p. 224), and he answered by noting how often men's fantasies and male-oriented pornography entail an objectification of women who oftentimes are portrayed as powerless, dominated, belittled, humiliated, posessed, and harmed, which is a turn on for men and attests to the centrality of male aggression and hostility. While Stoller considered fantasies perverse, other authors were inclined to only consider the enactment of fantasies perverse. Masud Khan (1979) opined: "pervert [sic] phantasies without practice do not constitute perversion" (p. 121, italics added) and in her 1995 book, which she dedicated to Robert Stoller, Joyce McDougall opined: "In my opinion, the only aspect of a fantasy that might legitimately be described as perverse would be the attempt to force one's erotic imagination on a non-consenting or non-responsible other... Perhaps in the last resort, only relationships can aptly be termed perverse" (p. 177, italics added).

It is widely known that perverse practices and perverse fantasies are much more characteristic of men than of women. Perverse sexual practices—blatant genital exhibitionism, voyeurism, fetishism, frotteurism, pedophilia, and so on and so forth—are almost exclusively male proclivities. Such practices and proclivities tend to interfere with the perverse individual's ability to directly experience the raw reality of the sex partner's otherness—her subjectivity, the particulars of her existence that set her apart from all other women. Fetishization—a core manifestation of perversity—takes shape, for example, when a man zeroes in on a woman's breasts, turning her into nothing more than a pair—which perhaps are better than other such pairs—but, at the same time, no different as well, seeing that every woman is comparably equipped. Fetishization can have the effect of blocking sight of the essential aspects of a woman's being. As a result, a part (breasts) substitutes for the whole of her—a retreat from whole-object type relations.

Stoller (1985b) saw perversion as a "solution to a failure of intimacy" (p. 43). For perverse individuals, noted Khan (1979), "there is no possibility of true relating or mutuality" (p. 16)—only a "charade" of intimacy. The perverse individual does not surrender to a mutual (truly intersubjective) interpersonal process. He is incapable of "object-relatedness" (p. 23) and, instead, treats others like "transitional objects" (p. 25). These observations led Khan to liken perversity to a manic defense that "enables the ego to avoid abject helplessness and threat of dissolution and disintegration as well as depression" (p. 27).

The topic of perversion is complex and not only covers perversions proper (perverse practices, such as voyeurism or exhibitionism), but it also covers the role and function of sexual fantasies (spelled with an "f" rather than a "ph" to distinguish the former—which is conscious—from the latter, which is unconscious), perverse thinking (a failure to face facts, difficulties with reality), perverse modes of relating to others (objectifying or fetishizing others), and perverse character structure (tendencies to play with another's sense of reality). Together, these topics represent much of what interested Stoller and much of the content contained in the books and papers he wrote.

Fetishization

Fetishes tend to be objects or conditions that become inserted into one's sexual dealings with others. At the most extreme end of the perverse spectrum, the self itself may be taken as object (Corrigan Herzog, 2004). One's involvement with a fetishistic object can go so far as to constitute one's primary object relationship—illustrated by a male patient described by Rubin (2025) whose fetishistic practices involved the solitary use of chastity belts that had the effect of heightening his sexual arousal, creating what the patient referred to as his "universe of one." The patient used these fetishes in ways that suggested they served as a transitional object for him—an eroticized version of the physical restraints his cold and distant mother used to control him as a child, treating him as if a dog on a leash.

The chief function of a fetish is to allay the individual's anxiety (e.g., to quell castration anxiety triggered by the sight of an absent penis) and/or help the individual manage the welling up of unbearable levels of trauma-related internal tension. A fetish is a sleight-of-hand, magical illusion that makes situations appear other than how they are. The fetish-using perverse individual knows and, at the same time, does not know the nature of things as they are.[3]

Fetishes tend to be concrete things, conditions, or storylines (fantasies) inserted into a scene to create the impression something is present that in fact is absent. A man requires his lover smoke a cigarette half believing cigarette = missing penis, which the man both knows and does not know to be missing. In fact, fetishization need not involve a concrete and tangible thing/object; fetishization can involve a distraction ("look at that ass!") used to keep oneself from focusing, for example, on the woman's missing penis, which triggers unbearable castration anxiety in some men. Fetishization can go as far as to involve another's entire being. A man, for example, ignores those particulars of a woman that make her who she is—her unique features that distinguish her from other women that save her from being turned into a stereotype.

There are instances when fantasies themselves, when inserted into a sexual scene, operate fetishistically. If a man is making love to one woman, for example, while imagining doing so with another woman, is this not a form of fetishization? Like all other fetishes, this represents something (the fetish) inserted into the sexual scene that interferes with the man's experiencing himself experiencing the woman he is with. Extending such thinking a bit further, we might ask whether a man who marries a string of look-alike women is essentially fetishizing the entire lot's surface appearances (Balint, 1956).

Pornography

Stoller was fascinated with the factors that make a sexual scene exciting for a specific individual. For Stoller, sexual arousal was all about the story: who the fantasizer imagines the other to be and what the unfolding events come to personally mean to him. Stoller called these stories "erotic plots," alternately referred to as sexual fantasies and sexual daydreams.

To unpack what a sexual scene might mean to a given individual, Stoller turned for help to the porn industry that was actively turning out product that was turning on men, who were the chief target audience. This isn't to say women don't also partake, it is only to note the erotic storylines that arouse men and women differ considerably. Stoller reasoned that no industry would survive let alone thrive, as the porn film industry was doing in the 1970s and 1980s, if its product didn't hit the spot by correctly identifying and catering to a wide range of male appetites.

Stoller quickly concluded that the specificity of a man's sexual fantasies serve as a sort of biopsy of the man's character. He realized how a man's pent-up aggression and hostility can effectively be discharged by watching porn that portrays his fantasies playing out. The sexualization of that hostility and aggression (the exciting wish to harm or control women) led Stoller to conclude that men's fantasies and the erotic plots of the porn men like to watch are perverse in nature to the extent they represent an expression of erotic (sexualized) hatred. By comparison, Milton Glasser, Head of London's Portman Clinic that specializes in the treatment of perversion, saw matters differently. Whereas Stoller saw male aggression primarily as a vengeful manifestation of a man's core sadism, Glasser saw male aggression, which becomes sexualized, as an attempt to protect self and other from the destructive effect of relating to others. In this book, Glasser's theories are presented alongside those of Stoller to note similarities and differences.

What most interested Stoller were the factors that helped shape a given man's unique proclivities. Stoller realized two chief roles that porn and fantasy serve: to permit a (questionably) societally acceptable outlet for the expression of a man's sadistic impulses toward women, which helps a man divert such impulses away from the woman with whom he is having sexual relations. Pornography and fantasy are vehicles that help men sequester the expression of their hostility and aggression, which they compartmentalize to prevent such potentially destructive impulses from damaging their relationships with a significant other. The other, perhaps more profound discovery Stoller made regarding the function of fantasy is the role early childhood trauma plays in helping shape a man's sexual fantasies and his attraction to watch certain pornographic themes. Such traumas are exemplified by instances when a boy had been cruelly teased by female caregivers for having proudly displayed his male behaviors.

What a man sees playing out on the screen or in his mind's eye, on the one hand, and what he will permit himself to do with the woman he loves and adores, on the other, are often unrelated matters. A woman who discovers her man's pornographic habit may become insulted and outraged that he would resort to what, in her opinion, amounts to a loathsome practice, which she believes amounts to the man turning away from her to sights that he finds more satisfying and exciting. The function porn often plays in a man's life is thoroughly detailed in a chapter solely dedicated to the exploration of that topic. Suffice it say, for many men porn and actual sexual encounters are only vaguely related matters.

Male Psychology

Stoller was amongst the first psychoanalysts to write about gender development and gender identity. He developed two concepts: one that has to do with a man's variable sense of masculinity, which he termed "gender identity;" the other having to do with the more binary matter of whether one experiences oneself male or female, which he called "core gender identity."

With respect to gender identity, male culture differs considerably from female culture in that it has a well-established hierarchical structure ("hegemonic masculinity," Connell, 1987) that succinctly spells out what constitutes the ideal, dominant form of masculinity, which is akin to alpha male behavior. Such stereotypic male behavior shades all alternate forms of masculinity, which are considered subordinate. By comparison, there are a myriad of ways women can be women without any one way seeming to completely epitomize femininity.

Stoller outlined the prevailing (1980s) rules about how men need to behave and not behave to earn them the right of be considered manly: "Be tough, loud, belligerent; abuse and fetishize women; find friendship only with men but also hate homosexuals; talk dirty; disparage women's occupations," to which he added what he considered proscribed male behavior: "The first order of business in being a man is don't be a woman."

In fact, most men have trouble maintaining a consistent, unwavering sense of themselves as manly men given the extent to which a man's sense of masculinity is vulnerable to being called into question by women and other men, which is not the case when to comes to women's sense of femininity. Many men feel their self-worth as men lies in the hands of the woman they desire, which contributes to men's dread of women (Horney 1932). Men challenge other men by testing to see whether they can withstand the pressure of being "razzed" by having their manhood challenged. The instability of a boy or man's sense of masculinity is one of the most consequential features of male psychology. Women, by comparison, are much more secure in their gender identity, which helps explains why they aren't nearly as threatened when they experience homo-erotic attraction.

To understand the vulnerability of a man's sense of masculinity requires we consider the path that leads boys to become gendered beings. Between 16–19 months of life, boys discover their penises and the implications of having one (Galenson & Roiphe, 1974, 1976). During this stage, boys are full of themselves and feel superior for being in league with those who are comparably endowed. The boy aggrandizes his penis and his body as well, which he loves to show off. These cocky boys, in look-at-me-look-at-me mode, proudly display themselves and their physical prowess, exhibitionism being a defining feature of the phallic narcissistic stage. They couldn't be happier about how things turned out, but they have a sobering and terrorizing thought: "If girls can lose their penises, so can I." The boy's discovery of his penis fills him not just with glee but also with a sense of dread.

There is a clear link between a boy's castration anxiety, his fear his penis will be taken from him, and his subsequent adult fear that he might be robbed of his ability to continue to feel sufficiently masculine. The fear of literal castration extends to a fear of metaphoric castration, the threat of being emasculated by those who traumatically mock his phallic displays, puncturing his inflation, resulting in a traumatic deflation. Simply put, boys and men feel they have a lot to lose and one way they compensate for such castration fears is to strut about in hyper-masculine fashion, making sure everyone sees they are complete and whole. Phallic narcissism amounts to a manic-like defense against feelings of weakness, lack, inadequacy, smallness and...need.

Stoller's outline of the societal dictates about what makes a man a manly man: ("Be tough, loud, belligerent; abuse and fetishize women" and so on) could be considered these days to be an apt description of what colloquially has come to be known as "toxic masculinity." Toxic masculinity most likely represents a fixation at or regression to the phallic narcissistic stage of development. Men who fail to outgrow this stage are at risk from becoming toxically masculine men. The following list spells out the behaviors, attitudes, and beliefs that characterize toxic masculinity. Such men are inclined to:

1   Resort to violence and aggression.
2   Strive for power and status, using a winner-take-all mindset.
3   Dominate and control others.
4   Display misogyny in their attitudes, language, or actions.
5   Exaggerate toughness and bravado to project hypermasculinity.
6   Project smug self-satisfaction, arrogance, and superiority.
7   Assume a "know it all" attitude, believing they can tell others how they should be and how they should act.
8   Act entitled, taking without asking, doing as one pleases.
9   Lack humility, averse to admitting errors or accepting blame.
10 Deny weakness or vulnerability.
11 Stoically suppress tender emotions.
12 Reject help from others to uphold the ethos that men must be strong, independent, and entirely self-sufficient.

Before we move on and describe Robert Stoller, the man, it is important to acknowledge that Stoller's theories have been challenged and are presently considered by some to have been disproven. In the final chapter, this topic will be discussed in detail. The dismissal of Stoller's thinking is uncalled for given the lack of evidence that supports such claims. Those gender theorists who follow Jean Laplanche have parlayed his theories into what they believe to be a substantial challenge to the bulk of Stoller's ideas about gender and gender identity, but their writings contain serious flaws in reasoning, as will be demonstrated.

Robert Stoller

Many present-day analysts may be unfamiliar with the writings of Robert Stoller, despite the fact his novel and controversial theories galvanized the psychoanalytic community decades ago. Over time, many of the field's best minds felt obliged to comment on his work, whether they supported his conclusions, took issue with them, or used them to build or support theories of their own. Those who weighed in included such luminaries as Janine Chasseguet-Smirgel, Jean Laplanche, Jessica Benjamin, Andrea Celenza, Nancy Chodorow, Micheal Diamond, Eleanor Galenson, André Green, Adrianne Harris, Ethel Person, Avgi Saketopoulou, and many more.

Stoller's work upended many classical psychoanalytic theories about gender identity, the nature of the erotic lives of humans, sexual fantasy, sexual excitement, and a slew of other related topics. He called upon analysts to rethink their core concepts about sexuality, to move from conceptualizing sexual desire as a somatic craving—a "drive"—to make space for the realization one's sexual appetites—memorialized in one's favored fantasies—represent a "drama" of sorts—a drama endlessly enacted to help the individual come to terms with childhood frustration and childhood traumas of one sort or another.

André Green (2001) drives home the role Stoller's thinking played in the evolution of psychoanalytic thinking about sexuality, calling Stoller's work "the only important advance in the field since Freud . . . [it] cannot be understood as a simple addition to Freudian theory of sexuality. It constitutes one of the most powerful reasons for reconsidering the foundations on which that theory rests" (p. 31). In her review of his 1985 book *Presentation of Gender*, Eleanor Galenson (1985) refers to Stoller as "one of the most out-standing contributors to the study of human sexuality" (p. 1075).

Laplanche credited Stoller both for recognizing the development of gender takes place earlier than most had thought (before the onset of the Oedipal phase of development) and for asserting that one's sense of maleness is pre-dicated on both the post-delivery gender assignment as well as conscious and preconscious parental attitudes about maleness and sexuality that get transmitted to the young child by his parents.[4]

An important advancement in our thinking about gender that Stoller helped facilitate is a distinction that people now take for granted. These days, people by and large understand the difference between gender identity (whether one feels oneself male or female) and the gender of the person one feels attracted to and wishes to have sexual relations with (one's sexual object choice). My own under-standing about such matters was informed by evaluations I was conducting in the 1980s with individuals wishing to undergo gender reassignment surgery. Stoller referred these individuals to a team that was performing the evaluations surgeons required before they were willing to conduct surgery, and I was the psychiatrist who was conducting the psychiatric portion of the pre-surgical evaluation. One such individual—born female—told me that he (here, I will use the pronoun that is consistent with the patient's core sense of gender identity) had always felt himself to be very much male; accordingly, he was seeking to undergo surgery to provide him with a penis-like organ of his own. As for how he planned to act once prop-erly outfitted, he was clear about his sexual preference. What he said has stuck with me to this day: he was planning to have sex with a man as a man. While readers today may knowingly shrug about what for me, at the time, was revela-tory, I see this as a measure of how far we have come in our thinking, in our understanding about these nuanced differences.

Some Final Comments

Stoller's research into fantasy, fetishization, and perversion was not chiefly con-ducted with patients he was seeing; one gets the impression his clinical practice was limited relative to his colleagues who were in private practice. Stoller took as much time as he needed to conduct in-depth interviews with a host of individuals living lives that were far from ordinary: members of the S&M subculture, dominatrixes, individuals with a variety of unusual sexual proclivities. He studied "want ads" from pornographic magazines (man seeking cigar-smoking woman, forced enemas, golden showers, tickling victims, amputee lovers, and so on and so forth) and the varied storylines of pornographic magazines and movies. He conducted lengthy interviews with writers, actors, and producers who were hard at work crafting pornographic films that would appeal to men of various sorts and proclivities.

Interviewing those engaged in the production of pornographic films provided Stoller a window into the erotic lives of human beings in general. The results of this research are chiefly contained in three volumes: *Porn: Myths for the Twentieth Century* (Stoller, 1993), *Coming Attractions: The Making of an X-rated Movie.* (Stoller & Levine, 1993), and *Sweet Dreams, Erotic Plots: A Previously Unpublished Work by Robert Stoller* (Stoller, 2009).

Stoller's research methods resembled those employed by cultural anthropologists and ethologists. He maintained a close collegial bond with one of his mentees, Gilbert Herdt, a postdoc in psychiatry who had been conducting field research with the Sambia tribe that lived in an isolated region of Papua New Guinea. In 1979, Stoller flew in a single-engine plane to the grassy airstrip located a grueling, two-hour hike from the remote village where Herdt was conducting his fieldwork (Herdt, 2020). Together, he and Herdt spent ten days conducting intimate interviews with several tribesmen whose trust they earned, resulting in the publication of a co-authored article, "The development of masculinity: A cross-cultural contribution" (Stoller & Herdt, 1982) and a co-authored book *Intimate Communications: Erotics and the Study of Culture* (Herdt & Stoller, 1990).

The other matter worth mentioning before completing this introduction has to do with Stoller's writing style, which reviewers praise as being to the point, easy to read, unpretentious, engaging, and eloquent. In reviewing Stoller's work, Fisher (1996) opined: "Rather than reciting old platitudes or warmed-over formulas about sexuality, Bob restored sexuality to its rightful subversive place in the psychoanalytic understanding of the individual (p. 7). Though Laplanche (2011a) was critical of many of Stoller's conclusions, he had to admit that Stoller's work demonstrated a "strikingly impressive freedom of style" (p. 181); and, in reviewing Stoller's (1985) *Observing the Erotic Imagination*, Gedo (1988) opined "Stoller has produced a devastating polemic against the dogmatic misuse of theory, the obfuscatory functions of unnecessary jargon, and the illegitimate construction of fictive entities through overgeneralization from limited samples" (p. 529).

What I find particularly appealing about Stoller's writing is the way he plays with language and his dedication to take care not to hide behind concepts that imply he knows more about a matter than can be known. In a word, I find his writing "refreshing." His style of writing contributes greatly to how I aspire to write. In writing this book, I re-read nearly everything

Stoller wrote about the topics of perversion, gender identity, the development of a sense of masculinity and femininity, fetishization, sexual excitement, and pornography; and, while this book's aim is to do what Stoller failed to do—to explicate a robust theory about the psychological and emotional development of the male species—the scope of the book is not limited to his writings alone. His theories are contextualized by reviewing what many other contemporary analysts theorized about these topics.

Notes

1 Stoller (1975) dedicated an entire chapter (Variants: Aberrations That Are Not Perversions") to drive home this point.
2 "Arbus made her intense relationship with the people she photographed the subject of her work—her curiosity about the details of their lives, their willingness to share their secrets and the thrilling discomfort she felt during these encounters ... This sense of mutuality is one of the most striking and original things about Arbus' photographs, giving them a lucidity and focus that are as much psychological as photographic ... The challenge, she wrote, was 'not to ignore them, not to lump them all together, but to watch them, to take notice, to pay attention'" (DeCarlo, 2004), which is the antithesis of fetishization.
3 Laplanche (2011a) writes: "I have never said—I do not think I ever said—that there are unconscious messages from parents. On the contrary, there are conscious/preconscious messages and that the parental unconscious is like the 'noise'—in the sense of communication theory—that comes to perturb and to *compromise* the conscious/preconscious message" (p. 175). This clarification aims to correct those who read Laplanche as speaking of the transmission of unconscious thoughts and feelings about sexuality and masculinity.
4 For example, an individual claims he doesn't want the listener to "get the wrong impression" that he is being, for example, critical of the listener, so he prefaces his veiled remarks by saying "with all due respect," which hides the fact he is about to launch into a disrespectful critique. A statement that uses negation both acknowledges and negates the same claim.

About the Author

Richard Tuch is a Volunteer Clinical Professor of Psychiatry at the David Geffen School of Medicine, University of California, Los Angeles (UCLA). He is a Training and Supervising Analyst at The New Center for Psychoanalysis (Los Angeles) and the Psychoanalytic Center of California (Los Angeles). He is former head of the Scholarship Section of the Department of Psychoanalytic Education, a division of The American Psychoanalytic Association. He serves on two editorial boards: the *Journal of the American Psychoanalytic Association* and *The Psychoanalytic Quarterly*. Many of his articles and book reviews appear in a variety of peer-reviewed psychoanalytic journals, and he has written and co-written several books and book chapters. His interest in the work of Robert Stoller is directly related to personal experiences he had being taught by Professor Stoller when he was in psychiatric training at UCLA.

1 Being a Gendered Being
Maleness versus Manliness

This book is about men: men who think of themselves as men, men who possess a solid sense of their gender, men convinced—beyond a shadow of a doubt—that they are men; yet men—nonetheless—who know they have a lot to lose, and may behave in ways designed to telegraph their indisputable masculinity in reaction-formation like fashion (Person & Ovesey, 1983). Possessing an unwavering internal sense of one's maleness, on the one hand, and performing masculine displays (e.g., peacocking), on the other, are two distinct aspects of gender—*maleness versus masculinity*–the former Stoller referred to as *core gender identity*, the latter he simply called *gender identity*. Present-day gender theorists dispute the legitimacy of both these categories of gender identity, which will be taken up and discussed in this book.

Given the centrality of the notion of gender in the zeitgeist, it is somewhat surprising to realize the topic of "gender" was not analytically addressed until mid-century,[1] when John Money began scientifically considering the topic from a behavioral point of view (Money et al., 1955a, 1955b, 1957). It was Money who introduced the term "gender role" (distinct from Stoller's term "gender identity") to designate outward displays of masculinity—the performance of gender versus gender as an internal conviction. Money (1973, p. 3) describes gender role as involving the following features:

> general mannerisms, deportment, and demeanor; spontaneous topics of talk in unprompted conversation and casual comment; content of dreams, daydreams, and fantasies; replies to oblique inquiries and projective tests; evidence of erotic practices and, finally, the person's own replies to direct inquiry.

Gender role, as defined by Money, is the empirical, behavioral manifestation of gender: the observable qualities or attributes that are characteristic of boys and men. Such displays differ from *core gender identity*, a term introduced into the psychoanalytic lexicon by Stoller (1964, 1965, 1973, 1979, 1985a; Stoller & Wagonfeld, 1982). Core gender identity refers to an internal (private) sense of maleness that can only be construed inferentially

DOI: 10.4324/9781003609339-1

(Person & Ovesey, 1983). Here, we are differentiating maleness (*core* gender identity) from masculinity (gender identity)—the difference between a durable conviction that one is male, on the one hand, versus either observable masculine displays of stereotypic male behaviour, or a personal sense of feeling varying degrees of masculinity, on the other.

Though we speak today of the existence of non-binary gender identity to acknowledge and respect the subjectivity of a select group of individuals, most humans do not question whether they are male or female. Surprisingly, some present-day gender theorists believe gender is universally non-binary, but assuming what is true for a few is true for one and all is a stretch that negates the experience of those who have never doubted whether they are male or female. As for a man's sense of masculinity, it is now widely accepted that experiencing oneself as masculine "through and through" tends only to be seen in men who manifest a *rigid* sense of masculinity—men incapable of locating anything within them that smacks of femininity, anything that threatens the man by dint of his feeling weak or needy.

In his paper "The Sense of Maleness," Stoller (1965) wrote:

> By the sense of maleness I mean the awareness, "I am a male." This essentially unalterable *core of gender identity* is to be distinguished from the related but different belief, "I am manly (or masculine)." The latter attitude ["gender identity"] is a more subtle and complicated development. It emerges only after the child has learned how his parents expect him to express masculinity, that is, to behave as they feel males should. (p. 207, italics added)

This passage adds an important element by addressing the role environment plays (e.g., parental attitudes about how they want their boys to be and to act; a mother's seductive attempt to keep her son extra close) in helping shape a boy's sense that he is both male (quality) and to some degree masculine (quantity).

For Stoller (1976a), *gender identity* inherently involved a *"mix of masculinity and femininity found in every person ... [whereas] core gender identity develops first and is the central nexus around which masculinity and femininity gradually accrete"* (p. 61, italics added). Gender identity (masculinity) manifests either as the outward display of stereotypical behaviors thought to be indicative of men or as a personal sense of one's manliness (the male "role")—both of which, Stoller noted, can be seriously shaped (or damaged) either by the way caretakers treat the child (e.g., by dressing him in girls' clothes) or by what they subliminally communicate to the child about what they expect of the child or what they can tolerate in the way of the child's masculine displays.

Saketopoulou and Pellegrini (2023) take aim at Stoller's concept of *core gender identity*, which they declare to be "at best simplistic and at worst problematic" (p. xxii). They noted that gender is "not about some ontologically true interiority" (p. xxix); rather, it should be seen as something fluid—as if in a perpetual state of "becoming," not something set in stone once and for all. The problem with their critique lies in their failure to differentiate between Stoller's two concepts, core gender identity and gender identity, which leaves readers confused about whether they are referring alternatively to one's sense of being, for example, male versus female or one's sense of being masculine or feminine, which Stoller goes out of his way to make clear that everyone's gender identity contains an admixture of both masculine and feminine aspects.

Stoller's Developmental Model

Stoller (1968) acknowledged the "bedrock" role that the resolution of the Oedipus Complex plays in establishing a boy's gender identity—his sense of masculinity. The boy's investment in his penis—the physical pleasure he gets from it, his pride in possessing it—is challenged on two fronts: the potential threat of castration and the need to come to terms with the "facts of life"—that the boy's wish to have mommy all to himself is doomed from the start. Freud's theory of gender identity—though not explicitly framed by him as such, seeing that there is no word for gender in the German language for gender—is predicated on the phallocentric belief that penis-endowed humans are complete and superior in comparison to humans who are not similarly endowed, who lack a penis and, according are "deficient" or "lacking."

In Freud's Oedipal stage schema, castration anxiety (the prospect of losing one's penis, literally or metaphorically) plays a central role in shaping the boy's sense of masculinity, while penis envy does likewise for the girl's developing sense of femininity. Freud further posited that the developmental path for girls is complicated by their having to switch love objects (from mother to father)—a task boys are spared, seeing that their ultimate love object (in the heterosexual model) is gendered in the same way that mother is gendered. The resolution of the Oedipus Complex contributes to the formation of the boy's sense of masculinity through his identification *with* the father who becomes his "pal"[2]—an identification that helps pull the boy out from the gravitational pull of the mother. Diamond (2006) noted:

> Through the boy's relationship with a father (or father surrogate) whom he admires, and who interacts with and mentors him in a caring way ... the boy is able to internalize a paternal imago ... the father's parenting becomes a foundation for healthy and fluid masculine gender identity. (pp. 1116–1117)

Diamond (2021) identifies Stoller's theory (specifically, his hypothesis about the boy's task of dis-identifying with the mother) as the underpinning of what Diamond refers to as the second wave of analytic theorizing about the development of a sense of masculinity, with the first wave being Freud's theory of the Oedipus Complex with its accompanying castration anxiety and penis envy, and the ultimate resolution of the Oedipus Complex, which is now assumed to never be fully complete. Diamond (2021) identified the work of Stoller et al. (Greenson, 1968; Stoller & Herdt, 1982) as upending Freud's assertion that the developmental path by which girls develop their gender identity is more complicated than the path taken by boys. Stoller (1974a) describes a problem that is unique to boys versus girls as they attempt to separate from their mother:

> Some of us believe (Greenson, 1968; Stoller, 1968) that, contrary to Freud's position ... the little boy, not the little girl, has the more devious route toward an intact gender identity in the first year or two of life. We believe that because little boys spend their most profoundly intimate experience up against a female body and psyche, they are at special risk of first identifying with that femaleness ["protofemininity"] and then of *not being able adequately to end that identification* by the creation of masculinity. (p. 211)

Stoller advanced two notions: Boys develop an unquestioning (fixed) conviction about their maleness at an early age—long before the onset of the Oedipal stage (3–5 years of age), which was a novel proposition at the time. Stoller further noted that a boy can have an unwavering conviction he is a boy *even if that boy lacks a penis*—instances when a boy is designated male at birth (the "sex assignment") and is raised indisputably as male by his parents who treat the penis-lacking boy as a boy nevertheless (Stoller, 1965). Rather than agree that "anatomy is destiny" (Freud, 1924), Stoller left space for the effect consciously and unconsciously held parental attitudes about gender and sexuality can have on the boy's developing sense of himself as male, as masculine, and as a sexual being—an idea later elaborated and championed by Jean Laplanche (2011a).

Having proposed a path to account for how a boy develops a sense of maleness (*core* gender identity), Stoller (1985a) next outlined a path by which a boy develops his sense of masculinity (gender identity):

> Wherein the boy is merged with mother ... lays the groundwork for an infant's sense of [proto]femininity. This sets the girl firmly on the path to femininity but puts the boy in danger of building into a core gender identity a sense of oneness with mother (a sense of femaleness). Depending on how and at what pace a mother allows her son to separate, this phase of merging will leave residual effects that may be expressed as disturbances in masculinity. (p. 16)

Writing in collaboration with his mentee Gilbert Herdt (an anthropology postdoc), Stoller proposed a stage of development they referred to as "protofemininity"—a stage during which the boy imagines himself to be merged with mother and, as a result, female like mother (Stoller & Herdt, 1982). This stage predates the development of the boy's sense of masculinity ushered in when the boy realizes and acknowledges he and his mother are not, never were, and never will be "one and the same" given their bodily differences. Forevermore, the boy's penis will set him apart from his mother; the illusion of merger is no more, and furthermore cannot be resurrected.

This realization sets in motion a developmental task that Stoller and Herdt refer to as the boy's "dis-identifying" from his mother—a concept borrowed from Ralph Greenson, who developed that "hypothesis," as he called it, when treating a single patient—a "transsexual-transvestite" 5-year-old boy named Lance (Greenson, 1966, 1968). The Stoller-Greenson-Herdt psychoanalytic model (the protofemininity/dis-identification hypothesis) was offered to account for the development of a boy's sense of masculinity. That hypothesis posits that a failure to dis-identify from mother arises from two sources: one related to the intensity of the boy's own urge to remain within the mother's orbit; the other having to do with the mother's powerful desire to maintain a tight bond with her son:[3] "To the extent [the boy's merger with mother] is intensified by having been encouraged too much," noted Stoller and Herdt (1982),

> the sense of being like her—identified with her—interferes with his masculinization. The boy who does not value masculinity—*in whom it has not been encouraged*—will have little reason to resist his sense of femininity and of being at one with his mother's femaleness. (pp. 31–32, italics added)

Comparing aspects of the first and second waves of analytical theorizing about the development of a sense of masculinity leads us to note that the first wave (Oedipal model) emphasized the father's role in helping draw the boy out from the gravitational pull of the mother, whereas the second wave (protofemininity/dis-identification hypothesis) highlighted *the boy's own struggle* to break free of the mother's hold over him and/or his own urge to stay merged with her. Furthermore, while Freud's model posited the girl's gender-related developmental path to be more complicated (predicated on a sense of lacking something essential combined with the need to switch love objects), the model proposed by Stoller, Herdt, and Greenson turned things upside-down: It is boys who not only must traverse a more challenging developmental pathway (dis-identifying *and remaining dis-identified*) but must also contend with their envy of the creative and nurturing powers of women (Greenson, 1968).

Supportive Evidence: Herdt's Anthropological Discoveries

To support the protofemininity/dis-identification hypothesis, Stoller drew upon the anthropologic fieldwork Herdt was conducting with the Sambia tribe—a Stone-Age hunting and horticultural community that lived in the remote and rugged mountains of Papua New Guinea (Stoller, 1985a; Stoller & Herdt, 1982). Sambia boys maintain a warm and tight bond with their mothers and have little contact with their fathers during the first seven years of their lives. With father out of the way, boys have unimpeded access to their mothers. The boys breastfeed into their third year of life and experience an abundance of skin-to-skin contact with their mothers. Mothers treat their sons in a more indulgent manner relative to their daughters. Sons are pampered and spoiled, and are permitted to be more demanding of the mother than their sisters, who, by comparison, are not to make a fuss if their wishes are thwarted.

When the boy comes of age (roughly seven years old), all contact with the mother is abruptly terminated. Boys are separated from their mothers and undergo initiation rites culminating in their becoming inducted into the ranks of men. Radical and brutal methods are used to sever ties between the boy and his mother, with strict sanctions levied should the boy talk with, touch, or even look at his mother. Continued contact is culturally deemed to threaten the emergence of the boy's nascent manhood. A clear message is transmitted: Women pollute and deplete, which threatens the boy's burgeoning masculinity. Boys must become strong, warrior men who stand ready to battle and kill members of impinging tribes.

Having spent years closely tied to their mothers, Sambia boys are culturally deemed to be lacking in a requisite masculine-dependent substance, which they receive from teenage boys by ingesting their semen; fellatio is an institutionalized part of the initiation rite. The younger boys receive "masculinizing semen" from teenage bachelor males. Then, once they themselves have entered adolescence, they provide semen to new initiates coming up the ranks. Such practices culminate in exclusively adult heterosexual practices.

The Implications of Herdt's Work

It is easy to distance ourselves from such primitive thinking; but, if we are honest, we will recognize elements of such thinking in our own culture. Stoller outlined the types of attitudes present-day men are expected to have to establish themselves as sufficiently differentiated from the young, feminized boy they once had been—a boy enamored and identified with his mother. Stoller spells out the male ethos: "Therefore, be tough, loud, belligerent; abuse and fetishize women; find friendship only with men but also hate homosexuals; talk dirty; disparage women's occupations. The first order of business in being a man is: don't be a woman" (Stoller & Herdt, 1982, p. 34). Stoller (1985a) asserted: "For much of masculinity, as is well known, consists of struggling not to be seen by oneself or others as having feminine attributes, physical or psychological. One must maintain one's distance from women or be irreparably infected with femininity" (p. 18).[4] Today, we associate such thinking with toxic masculinity, but that was not the case a half century ago when Stoller was doing little more than articulating what every man seemed to know and believe, echoed by Person and Ovesey (1983): "In this view of gender development, the bedrock of feminine identification means that all men must struggle to overcome a feminine identification. Men, therefore, in general, are more susceptible to problems in gender identity than women" (p. 214).

The problem with extending observations about the Sambia people to Western civilization lies in the noteworthy differences in how each culture raises children. There is no "Oedipal bed" in Sambia culture, given that boys sleep naked with their mothers until the age of seven, with father largely out of sight, relegated to different rooms of the house and different areas of the village. While Western children are confronted with Oedipal issues at around 4–5 years of age, Sambia boys remain closely bound to their mothers until seven, which makes a world of difference.

Challenging the Protofemininity/Dis-identification Hypothesis

The protofemininity/dis-identification hypothesis suggested that if the door is left ajar and the boy yields to the temptation to regress—to metaphorically return to the breast—his nascent and tenuous sense of masculinity is at risk (Diamond, 2021). To protect against such a calamity, the proto-femininity/dis-identification hypothesis stipulates that men must sever ties, doing so to the extent of erasing *any vestige* of femininity that lies within, the legacy of their bond with mother. They may also become hostile to females in general, not just to the feminine within,[5] and to effeminate men. Rather than risk being seen as a "momma's boy" or a "pussy," boys must make a clean break from mother and not fuss over the loss. After all, boys don't cry. Diamond (2006) notes "the young boy is culturally prohibited from knowing or valuing his loss and coerced to deny his need for his mother" (p. 1122).

Though the protofemininity/dis-identification hypothesis received strong anthropological support from Herdt's research and was largely accepted at the time, that hypothesis is now considered to have been disproven given research findings that discredits Mahler's (1975) concept of infant–mother symbiosis.[6] Laplanche (2011a) declared: "when the Mahlerian [symbiosis argument] foundation collapses ... the whole Stollerian etiology collapses" (p. 189). As we shall see, Laplanche was mistaken in the absoluteness of his declaration.

The infantile symbiosis argument against the protofemininity/dis-identification hypothesis is not the only, or even the most formidable, challenge to the standing of the hypothesis. That hypothesis posited that boys felt obliged not only to dis-identify from their mothers but also to *repudiate what they lost* in the process. That hypothesis failed to consider the possibility that some boys—perhaps most—subsequently regain the ability to feel identified with their mothers. Such boys evolve to the point they no longer feel as threatened by feeling identified with and close to their mothers as they once had felt. This is not to suggest *all* boys succeed in outgrowing the need to distance themselves from their mother or from mother substitutes. A regression to, or fixation at the stage of phallic narcissism is associated with a continued sense that one needs to keep women at bay lest one's masculinity becomes infected with femininity.

Diamond (2004a, 2004b, 2006, 2015) was amongst the earliest and strongest voices speaking in opposition to Stoller's concept of dis-identification. He argued that the stage during which the boy turns away from his mother is transient not permanent. Diamond argued the idea of an absolute ("forevermore") versus relative ("for the time being") repudiation of one's identification with mother and with women in general is deeply problematic. Such repudiation—spelled out in Stoller's quip "The first order of business in being a man is: don't be a woman"—suggests that men sustain their sense of masculinity by wiping out any vestige of internal femininity. "As long as gender identity is based on the disavowal of whatever is construed as feminine," noted Diamond (2015), "it remains a highly unstable psychological achievement" (p. 53).

The protofeminity hypothesis that posited both boys and girls initially experience themselves as female until they realize otherwise directly contradicts Freud's theory of *the primacy of masculinity*, with femininity developing in the wake of the little girl's "discovery of her organic inferiority" (Freud, 1931, p. 232) given the boy's "superior equipment" (Freud 1933, p. 126). This developmental stage occurs temporally coincident with the little boy's discovery that he has a penis while others don't and his fantasy that castration made it so, which leads a boy to "choose the narcissistic cathexis of his penis over the libidinal cathexis of his mother" (Person & Ovesey, 1983, p. 207), who he then renounces. Freud's developmental model must be amended to take into consideration evidence that a child's core gender identity is formed long before he or she reaches the Oedipal phase of development (Galenson & Roiphe, 1976), roughly when the child is 18 months of age.

Freud (1933) did not regard an individual's sense of femininity or masculinity binary the way he considered their sense of maleness and femaleness to be: "an individual is not a man or a woman but always both—merely a certain amount more the one than the other ... what constitutes *masculinity or femininity* is an unknown characteristic which anatomy cannot lay hold of" (p. 114, italics added). This last comment challenges the argument of present-day gender theorists who insist, despite evidence to the contrary, that Freud's thinking about gender was strictly anatomically based.

Challenging Freud's view of the primacy of masculinity does not, by exclusion, prove Stoller's theory that posited femininity ("proto" as it is) is the primary gender experienced both by girls and boys early in life. Stoller based his protofemininity theory on his work with transsexual patients whose condition he saw as the, outcome of a "biopsychic" process involving a mother who interacts with her son in ways that prolong their collective state of blissful union, resulting in the boy's becoming non-conflictually imprinted with femininity. Stoller (1976b) regarded his theory of transsexualism *"a key-stone for understanding the development of masculinity and femininity in all people* (p. 174, italics in original). Person and Ovesey (1983) considered Stoller's use of transsexualism dubious grounds upon which to theorize about the gender development of all boys and men, noting "there is no evidence that the symbiotic state that exists prior to self-object differentiation (here, falling in with Mahler's theory) is one of primary identification that confers gender behavior or gender identity on the infant child" (p. 125). These authors went a bit further by noting "there is no evidence that the original (or natural) gender state is masculine, as proposed by Freud, feminine, as suggested by Stoller, or that gender is innate, as proposed by Homey and Jones. Normal core gender identity arises from the sex of assignment and rearing. It is nonconflictual and is cognitively and experientially constructed. On the other hand, gender role identity, both normal and aberrant, is shaped by body, ego, socialization and sex-discrepant object relations. Unlike normal core gender identity, it represents a psychological achievement and is fraught with psychological conflict" (p. 222).

Phallic Narcissism in Adulthood

A persistence of phallic narcissism into adulthood manifests in displays of "hypermasculinity": bravado, arrogance, omnipotence, exhibitionism, (displays of strength and ablility that seek to garner attention and adoration), tendencies to dominate, and so on. Such patients exhibit "an excess of self-satisfaction" (Corbett et al., 2014; Diamond, 2006) that is characteristic of the state of phallic narcissism. The boy's confidence that he is in possession of what he deems the "superior organ," is a line of thinking Diamond (2006) refers to as "phallic monism"—the belief that the penis is *the* sexual organ, which helps the boy defensively avoid recognizing any sense of lack or deficiency (see Chasseguet-Smirgel, 1976; Figlio, 2010) or vulnerability relative to the inherent instability of his sense of masculinity. It is worth considering the extent to which the concept of "penis envy," which arguably has merit, nevertheless can serve to protect the narcissistic equilibrium of men who harbor feelings that leave them feeling small, inadequate, and not "up to snuff." Phallic narcissism amounts to a manic-like defense against feelings of weakness, lack, inadequacy, smallness, and … need.

Phallic narcissism runs the gamut from instances that are temporary and tempered to perverse and malignant. We forgive the young boy who feels full of himself—proud to be toting a penis. We recognize what he is struggling to juggle the loss of closeness with mother, the narcissistic injury of lacking what it would take to be more like her and/or have her to himself, his envy of the mother, and an upsurge of reactive aggression that is mitigated—in part—by his swollen narcissism–his male pride–which is transparently vulnerable to being punctured and deflated—thus contributing to the instability of his sense of masculinity.

Phallic narcissists are individuals who exhibit a misogynistic mode of relating to their objects, have trouble forming and maintaining close intimate bonds, and fail to be able to recognize others for who they are and what they need or desire. Abraham (1917) described such men by noting: "Their true love-object is themselves ... [they have] a particularly high and abnormally emotional estimation of the penis ... [such men] takes revenge on every woman for the disappointments of love to which as a child his mother subjected him" (p. 297). Such hostility often manifests clinically in the form of transference reactions that are hard, if not impossible, to treat given the patient's insufferable and off-putting, contempt-ridden rivalry with the analyst, and the intensity of his demand and expectation to be loved (Horney, 1936). For such patients, "to change, to receive help, implies weakness," noted Rosenfeld (1987, p. 112):

> [This] is experienced as wrong or as failure by the destructive narcissistic organization which provides the patient with his sense of superiority. In cases of this kind there is a most determined chronic resistance to analysis, and only the very detailed exposure of the system enables analysis to make some progress.

In the End, Stoller Was Both Right and Wrong

This brings us to what, in my mind, is a most interesting juncture. Research supports the idea that Stoller was both right and wrong: He was wrong regarding the particulars of the *protofemininity-dis-identification* hypothesis, but right with respect to his hypothesis that the developmental path is more challenging for boys than it is for girls, directly refuting Freud's claim.

Where did Stoller go wrong? First, he accepted the now-debunked concept of infantile symbiosis posited by Mahler. Next, he equated *symbiosis* with *identification*, which led him to propose boys not only identify early on with their mothers but also form a *gender-based* identification with them. If one simply substitutes "individuation" for "dis-identification," certain of the problematic aspects of Stoller's protofemininity/dis-identification hypothesis fall away. A final problem with Stoller's hypothesis is the fact he envisioned dis-identification as the central, normative event in the development of every boy's sense of masculinity, despite the fact the concept of dis-identification was based on a single case report of a non-normative 5-year-old boy treated by his colleague, Ralph Greenson.

Stoller also failed to consider the extent to which this proposed "dis-identification" exists along a continuum—in certain cases intense and prolonged, in other cases mild and short-lived. Stoller failed to take into consideration the possibility that dis-identification represented a *temporary*, stage-related need to turn away from mother for the time being—a need that can, and often does, give way during the next developmental phase (the genital phase), during which the need to dis-identify softens sufficiently to permit the boy to reconnect with his enduring identification with mother.

A proposed retrieval of the boy's ability to feel comfortably identified with his mother marks the third wave of analytic thinking regarding the development of male gender identity. Stoller failed to recognize that the *persistence* of extreme degrees of dis-identification ("the first order of business in being a man is: don't be a woman") is not a general feature of every man's sense of masculinity; rather, it represents the persistence of phallic narcissism into adulthood, which results in character-defining psychopathology that has nothing to do with an across-the-board development of a boy/man's gender identity—his sense of masculinity.

While Stoller got this detail of his proposed hypothesis wrong (that all boys not only must dis-identify but also must *stay dis-identified* from the mother), the essential aspect of his hypothesis was indeed correct: that both the establishment *and ongoing maintenance* of gender identity (feeling manly, in the case of boys and men) are considerably more challenging for boys than for girls, which makes a boy/man's sense of masculinity a highly unstable psychological achievement.

Stoller saw a man's sense of manliness/masculinity as vulnerable, which makes a man's dealings with women dicey: Not only do some men eschew internal femininity, but they also disrespect exterior femininity—femininity that takes shape in a woman's way of being. When a man's dread of women (Horney, 1932) becomes strong, given his need to avert the supposed weakening effects of experiencing his own interior receptivity (femininity), he develops contempt for women, expressed in his objectification and fetishization of them. Stoller saw man's fear of women as emanating from the combined effect of the potentially engulfing strength of a woman's incorporative desire, on the one hand, and the potentially obliterating strength of the man's wish to be one with mother/a woman, on the other.

An abundance of research supports Stoller's claim that the task of separating from mother is considerably more challenging for boys than it is for girls—the results of which are dramatic and help shape the contours of male psychology in a profound manner for the rest of a man's life. Diamond does an outstanding job of cataloging research evidence that demonstrates the arduous path of male psychological development,[7] a review that led him to posit:

> Consistent with my postulation of heightened primordial vulnerability among males, it seems that infant boys have a more limited capacity for self-regulation, are more impacted by infant-mother attachment failures in containment and regulatory functioning, and require earlier maternal (and/or paternal) co-regulation than do girls.
>
> (Diamond, 2015, p. 63.)

The Present State of Psychoanalytic Thinking about Gender

I will not go into detail at this point about the state of analytic thinking about gender; I leave that to the final chapter of the book that explores this topic at great length. I do feel a need to acknowledge my awareness that some present-day gender theorists see gender universally as both non-binary and fluid—ever changing, in a state of perpetual state of becoming. Such writers call into question the existence of any such thing as core gender identity and they have trouble imagining the existence of individuals who report possessing a solid and irrefutable sense of being gendered either male or female. What I will argue in the book's final chapter is the extent to which those who cannot imagine individuals who experience gender as binary fail to conflate *core gender identity* (one's sense of being a male or a female) and gender identity (the extent to which one feels oneself to be masculine or feminine).

Most people, I would submit, do in fact experience a solid sense of being either male or female. Common sense and personal experience declares this to be so. But declaring as much does not and should not deny or discount the experiences of those whose sense of gender is non-binary and is experienced as being perpetually in flux. Each camp must struggle to see matters from the other's perspective. Declaring gender to only be what one makes it out to be is deeply problematic; current thinking about gender had best not fall into the trap of itself becoming binary by virtue of arguing in an either/or fashion as if: "We are right about gender and those who think otherwise are dead wrong."

Those who feel a deep conviction that they are male or female through and through may have trouble imagining other humans who experience themselves differently. This presents a challenge not only for the field of psychoanalysis, but for the culture at large. We collectively must expand our ability to grapple with and tolerate otherness, otherwise we are at risk of negating the existence of a population of individuals who differ from us, which is unacceptable.

Notes

1   Freud had not written of "gender" per se, since the German word *Geschlecht* means both sex and gender, though he had specific ideas about what distinguished male and female behavior as defined by the active/passive dichotomy.
2   Considered a "counter-identification" in Stoller's dis-identification schema.
3   Though this conceivably could represent a projection of the boy's own urges.
4   I remember, when I was in seventh grade (aged 12 or 13), abruptly dropping the flute, which I was playing in the school orchestra, having gotten it into my head that it was a "girls'" instrument, unlike drums or brass, which were "boys'" instruments.
5   That is, during the phallic phase; though this goes unconsidered in Stoller's thinking.
6   See Axelrod, 1997; Benjamin, 1988, 1991, 1995; Christiansen, 1996; Diamond, 2004a, 2004b, 2006, 2015; Fast, 1984; Laplanche, 2011a; Person & Ovesey, 1983; Pollack, 1995, 1998.
7   See Drury et al. (2012); Kochanska et al. (2001); Martel et al. (2009); Tronick and Weinberg (2000); Weinberg et al. (2006); Zeanah et al. (2009).

2 The Realm of Perversity

Our understanding of perversions per se, and the realm of perverse phenomenon in general, is substantially informed by a distinction Freud drew between neuroses and perversions. Freud suggested neurotics know deep down what's what: they don't deny reality; they find defense-facilitated "work-arounds" that help them avoid a moment when they might come face to face with aspects of reality they fear and deeply doubt they can psychically handle. The neurotics' use of defense mechanisms—specifically, ones that don't unduly interfere with the individual's reality testing—is a major achievement. Perverse individuals, by comparison, do not accept reality as it is: they strive to distract themselves from noticing intolerable aspects of reality by using an alternate, illusory view of matters—using fetishes or fetishistic-like phenomena to solve the problem. A man terrorized by the sight of the woman's absent penis requires, for example, that his lover wear high heels, which serve as a "stand-in" for the missing penis, which is missing no more—or so the fetishist would like to think. Freud (1905) summed this up when he declared: *"Neuroses are, so to say, the negative of perversions"* (p. 165).

"In contrast with neurosis, in which the *forbidden wish is renounced* [repressed] out of concern that it is too dangerous to pursue gratification of the wish in reality," noted Grossman (1993), "in perversion the wish persists, and the *perception of reality is altered* through the mechanism of disavowal" (p. 423). In perversion, two realities co-exist: the reality of lack or absence; and visual "proof" that claims otherwise—a presence that serves to negate the absence (or, more to the point, distracts one from noting the absence) by representing that which is missing as if it were present (represented by a symbolic fetish that functions as a "stand-in"). It is a magic trick: "Now you don't see it, now you do"—a rabbit pulled out of a hat.

When one thinks of perversion, what typically comes to mind are a host of different perverse sexual practices (e.g., voyeurism, exhibitionism, pedophilia, fetishization, and so on and so forth). Beyond such perverse practices lie other categories of perverse phenomena that, taken together, constitute the realm of perversity: *perverse modes of thinking* (Sánchez-Medina, 2002; Zimmer, 2003); *perverse modes of relating* (Bach, 1991; Filippini, 2005;

DOI: 10.4324/9781003609339-2

Stein, 2005; Tuch, 2008, 2010); and *perverse character structure* (Arlow, 1971; Herzog, 2004; Lihn, 1970, 1971). Greenacre (1960) believed perversions involve all three of these specific though overlapping realms. Throughout this book, when reference is made to "perverse individuals," readers should keep in mind that perversity describes a realm of phenomena—a spectrum—that can be found manifesting to varying degrees. At one end of the spectrum are individuals who have a "touch" of perversity; at the other end are those who are plagued by a pervasive and obsessive involvement with fetishist practices or those whose character is unmistakably twisted by perversity.

Perverse thinking involves an "attack on truth" akin to Bion's concept of −K (Sánchez-Medina, 2002). It manifests as a refusal "to face reality squarely" (Arlow, 1971, p. 318):

> When confronted with reality the individual can feel secure only if he can *turn his attention* to some realistic external perception [something concrete, fetishistic] which is distracting and reassuring because it corresponds to his unconscious phantasy of a female with a phallus.
>
> (Arlow, 1971, p. 324, italics added)

Perverse modes of relating involve a part-object type orientation that results in one's treating others as objects that exist to satisfy one's own desires and needs. Objects are denied their subjectivity and their existence as autonomous beings with lives of their own. Perverse modes of relating involve a failure to recognize the otherness of others, a tendency to use others to satisfy one's own needs without regard for how the other feels or what it is they want or need (McDougall, 1995; Tuch, 2010), and the use of control in one's interactions with others (Herzog, 2004). What distinguishes the use of a fetish (e.g., a reliance on an anxiety-relieving object or the enactment of a perverse fantasy), on the one hand, from perverse relatedness, on the other, hinges on the nature of what is being defended against, the degree to which one's sense of reality is compromised by the tendency to disavow aspects of reality, and the degree to which the entirety of one's object relations becomes infused with hostility and a need to control (neutralize) the object. While castration anxiety underlies certain instances of perversity and fetishization, other anxieties and fears can also contribute. This point calls for an expansion of what perversity is thought to entail.

Perverse character structure is epitomized by the practices of compulsive liars and practical jokers (Arlow, 1971)—those who routinely "mess" with another's sense of reality and, in doing so, feel masterful tricking others into accepting their lies as fact. A fetishistic relationship with reality can manifest, for example, in the practice of telling petty lies or committing practical jokes or hoaxes—causing the other to momentarily accept fabrication as fact, as will be amply illustrated using clinical material in the following chapter. The trickster takes advantage of the trust of others who fall for his fabrications ("gotcha!"), thus reassuring the pervert that *he* is not the one at risk of being proven humiliatingly gullible. All of this is predicated on a doer/done (Benjamin, 1990), eat-or-be-eaten, zero-sum-game model of human interaction.

After Freud's initial theorizing about the nature of perversion, psychoanalytic thinking about perversity was advanced primarily by the work of five leading analytic theorists, each of whom contributed their own unique perspective on the subject. Robert Stoller was the first to meaningfully weigh in. He provided a theory, built in part, on his dis-identification hypothesis, which suggested reasons why some boys/men find their dealings with mothers, mother figures, and women in general particularly daunting—to wit, the vulnerability of a man's sense of masculinity that requires he establish himself as other than mother: "The first order of business in being a man is: don't be a woman" (Stoller & Herdt, 1982, p. 34). Stoller's (1975) theory of perversion was chiefly predicated on his belief that perversion constitutes "the erotic form of hatred"—hatred emanating largely from narcissistic childhood traumas suffered at the hands of caregivers who shamed or belittled the child. His view of perversion involved repetitive efforts to undo childhood trauma, which became memorialized in the form of a man's favored sexual fantasies that dramatize the situation using an erotic plot.

The second analyst who generated an elaborate theory of perversity was Mervin Glasser. While Stoller's development model of dis-identification viewed movement taking place *from fusion to separation,* Glasser's model pictured matters moving in the opposite direction, *from separation to fusion.* Glasser's theory can be summarized thusly: The individual's urge to merge generates intense annihilation anxiety (an existential threat, loss of self), which—in turn—begets *non-hostile* aggression (differing from Stoller) that aims to obliterate and negate this threat (i.e., the needed object, not one's urge) to ensure the individual's survival. Concern that this aggression might endanger the object one needs and upon whom one depends (the central concern of the depressive position) leads the individual to fashion a *perverse solution* to retain one's bond with the object and ensure one's ongoing existence. This is achieved through the process of sexualization. The non-hostile aggression is converted (sexualized) into sadism: "the intention to destroy [eliminate the threat to one's existence] is converted into the wish to hurt and control. In this way the object is preserved, and the viability of the relationship is ensured, albeit in sadomasochistic terms" (Glasser, 1986, p. 10). In that Stoller viewed perversion as the "erotic form of hatred," one sees how Glasser's model differs in this respect from what Stoller posited.

The third writer who theorized about perversity was Janine Chasseguet-Smirgel. Her theories involved the perverse individual's efforts to deny certain essential differences that reflect the nature of reality—how things are ("the order," the "status quo")—that the perverse individual intends to challenge and undermine (arguably establishing a reasonable definition of "queer"). The fourth theorists considered is Masud Khan (1979), who focused on maternal pathology when theorizing about the factors that contribute to the development of perversity. Khan suggested that the mothers of boys who go on to develop perversions fail to recognize and relate to the subjectivity of the boy as distinct from who she imagines and wishes the boy to be, which forces the boy to see himself through that lens, resulting in his becoming alienated from himself. A fifth theorist, Phyllis Greenacre, proposed the existence of pre-Oedipal fetishes triggered by trauma in the first 18 months of life, which predates the realization of anatomical gender differences between boys and girls.

Returning to Stoller

Stoller (1975) proposed that perversion represents "the erotic form of hatred," which can be seen manifesting both in the *perverse practices* of men who are dedicated to treating women in a hostile (hateful) fashion and in the hostile nature of men's fantasies and pornographic preferences, which reflect their efforts to torture, tease, manipulate, possess, demean, belittle, objectify, dehumanize, and—in whatever way—harm women. Stoller believed such fetishistic tendencies are the result of numerous factors: the man's efforts to comfortably distance himself from the mother's castrating clutches, his own self-endangering wish to merger with the mother or mother substitutes, and efforts to exact revenge for having been traumatized by women when he was young.

A man who fails to satisfactorily navigate the process of individuating from his mother most likely will be unable to comfortably identify with her once the temporary, stage-dependent need to distance himself from her passes. A persistent need to underscore the fact one is nothing like one's mother or other women translates into contempt for the feminine one implicitly senses to lie within, which spills over and becomes expressed toward women in general—individuals who possess the much-hated feminine ways of thinking, feeling, and being that such men are dedicated to eradicating in themselves. This is one essential root of misogyny. A man whose sense of masculinity feels susceptible to threats that might expose him as being "less than a man" often feels a need to make explicit just how manly he is, achieved by displaying exaggerated masculine traits, attitudes, and behaviors ("toxic masculinity"), the result of his obliterating anything within that "smacks" of "femininity."

The second element of Stoller's theory of perversity involves his belief that men treat women in a hateful way as an *act of retribution* for having been narcissistically injured at the hands of mothering figures who shamed or demeaned the boy—particularly if he was shamed for being a boy, shamed for his maleness or his displays of masculinity. The perverse individual ceases to be libidinally invested in his objects; instead, he dehumanizes them, which paves the way for him to express unmitigated hostility toward them. The object is demeaned, belittled, shamed, desecrated, humiliated, controlled, and—in the end—defeated.

Stoller's (1975) trauma-based theory of perversion (perversion = the erotic form of hatred) envisions perversion helping to transform childhood narcissistic trauma into adult triumph, following the formula: "I am humiliated; I discover revenge; I humiliate; I have mastered the past" (Stoller, 1991, p. 49). The emphasis Stoller placed on his trauma-based theory tended to cast his dis-identification/individuation theory of perversity into the shadows. That theory argued that the boy's task of individuating from mother is double trouble: not only does the boy need to separate from mother as a person, much in the same way girls must, but he also must grapple with an additional reality—the fact he and mother are bodied differently. Only in the posthumous publication of his previously unpublished works do we hear Stoller directly highlight the role a boy's difficulties individuating plays in perversity, echoing ideas Glasser proposed:

> The boy must erect a barrier between the desire to remain merged with mother and the desire to be a free-standing male. The perversion in men are, I believe, in part the manifestations of this continuing struggle. For in them can be found, often overtly and always in hidden form, statements—desires—that females are degraded and to be degraded … perversion develops and persists as an unending effort to break away from mother and yet stay in contact.
>
> (Stoller, 2009, p. 60, italics added)

Men whose impulses to objectify, demean, or control women are strictly confined to their fantasy life (or their preference for perverse pornography storylines) should not be deemed perverse, despite the fact Stoller thought otherwise. If a man relies on fantasies *that remain fantasies*, we need not judge him as harshly as we might a man whose perverse attitudes result in his treating women in a sadistic and objectifying manner. It is men who permit such impulses to gain greater rein, infesting the man's dealings with others, that we feel justified in calling him perverse.

The Work of Mervin Glasser

Mervin Glasser (1979, 1985, 1986, 1992) suggested perverse individuals experience an intense desire to obliterate differences between themselves and their objects—differences they see as standing in the way of their wish to merge with the object. Whereas Stoller envisioned the boy's *need to flee* the mother's individuation-blocking clutches, to break free of her possessive need for him, Glasser viewed the situation from an entirely different angle, as man's wish to merge/dread of becoming merged with the mother, which is experienced as an existential threat.

Mervin Glasser was a London-based psychoanalyst who served as chairman of the Portman Clinic in the 1970s and 1980s. That clinic specialized in treating patients whose perverse practices landed them on the wrong side of the law (exhibitionism, pedophilia, voyeurism, fetishism, sexualized murder, and so on and so forth). Glasser (1979, 1985) proposed what he referred to as the "core complex theory" to account for the root cause of perversity.[1] When a young boy's needs are deeply gratified by his mother, he may be left with a *persistent* longing to become one with her (or with women who represent her)—a longing he may experience throughout his lifetime. Such longings may persist if the boy failed to successfully navigate the developmental phase during which he was to have successfully individuated from his mother, which required he withdraw from her and cease to yearn for her having successfully mourned the loss of her as he had once experienced her.

Glasser (2003) saw perversion as predicated on "a deep-seated and perversive longing for an intense and most intimate closeness to another person [mother/lover], amounting to a 'merging,' a state of 'oneness,' a blissful union" (p. 284). He theorized that perverse individuals believe merger will result in a complete gratification of their needs and desires, eliminating any chance they might feel intolerable levels of deprivation or narcissistic mortification. But, as ideal as the merger solution seems, Glasser noted a rub: The solution comes at a price—merger threatens the individual's sense of autonomous existence (Donald Winnicott's [1971] "going on being"), generating annihilation anxiety. In response, the individual feels a need to flee, but that too comes at a price. Given such conditions, the perverse individual entertains two equally unfeasible solutions: either flee the scene (leaving the patient utterly alone, disconnected, living in a state of deprivation in an objectless world) or attack the source of the problem ("self-preservative aggression," which targets—with an intent to eliminate—the needed and desired object who is experienced as an existential threat). In that neither solution is tenable, the patient alternates between the two in a vicious cycle.[2] To protect the needed object, the potentially object-obliterating aggression is diverted (e.g., redirected at the self) and converted (via sexualization), resulting in aggression being converted into sadism: "the intention to destroy is converted into a wish to hurt and control" (Glasser, 2003, p. 287). This then accounts for the eroticization of man's hatred of/hostility toward women.

Glasser's *self-protection-based* theory of perversion (aggression that aims to fend off loss of self through merger) contrasts with Stoller's *trauma-based* theory of perversity: "I am humiliated; I discover revenge; I humiliate; I have mastered the past" (1991, p. 49). Stoller pictures aggression arising primarily in response to one's having been treated poorly during childhood by one's caretakers or by one's failure to adequately individuate from the mother, whereas Glasser's theory views aggression as arising from existential threats.

Glasser's theory addresses one of the most confusing aspects of perversity—how something that is not essentially sexual becomes sexual: the sexualization of hatred, a wish to dominate others, to exact revenge, to avoid intimacy—instances when such behaviors and/or fantasies do not represent a manifestation of a somatic (sexual) drive nor an attempt to satisfy a bodily need (Coen, 1981; Glasser, 1986; Goldberg, 1995; Parsons, 2000). Rather than being about sexual arousal and sensual pleasure, such sexualized behaviors and/or fantasies primarily serve defensive functions in situations where "defense has greater urgency and significance in the patient's motivational hierarchy than does sexual drive gratification" (Coen, 1981 p. 907). This is in line with Ruszczynski (2018, p. 26), who noted:

> Though it is tempting to think that sexual perversions are primarily sexual and driven by sexuality, they are better understood as activities that hijack sexuality … recruiting it to accomplish ends that are fundamentally aggressive and destructive, resulting in what Stoller calls "eroticized hatred."

While Glasser takes a detour through aggression on the way to sadism, Stoller goes there directly, bypassing any concern the fetishist may have that his aggressive/sadistic treatment of the object may destroy the object or drive him or her away. "The central issue in perversion," posits Stoller (1975), is the triumph that comes from "being in control while the other loses control" (p. 128).

It is worth noting that Stoller's original trauma-based theory of perversion failed to include his original theory about the boy's psychological challenges *individuating* from the mother in the first place (which contrasts with Glasser's theory of merger, of de-individuation). This oversight was not corrected in print until 18 years after Stoller's untimely death—appearing in *Sweet Dreams, Erotic Plots: A Previously Unpublished Work of Robert J. Stoller* (2009).

The Work of Janine Chasseguet-Smirgel

Janine Chasseguet-Smirgel was another author who contributed significantly to the field's understanding of perversion. One chapter in her book *Creativity and Perversion* (1985), entitled "A Psychoanalytic Study of 'Falsehood,'" demonstrates the extent to which her thinking aligns with that of Arlow (1971), amongst others, who collectively saw perversion as being about one's refusal to face reality head on. Chasseguet-Smirgel noted that an "erosion of the double difference between the sexes and the generations" (1985, p. 2) constitutes the pervert's chief objective, resulting in chaos and the dismantling of the status quo—the "order"—resulting, for example, in the disavowal of the father's genital capacity (hence, the boy has nothing to envy; in fact his penis is *superior* to that of the father) and the creation and maintenance of an illusion that the boy is a more adequate partner for his mother: "his pregenitality [is] idealized (worshipped) by his mother [as] superior to his father's genitality" (p. 78). If that isn't perverse, I don't know what is.

Chasseguet-Smirgel cited the writings of the Marquis de Sade (1966), which she read as calling for

> the abolition of "children" as a category and "parents" as a category [along with] breaking down the barriers which separate man from woman, child from adult, mother from son … [destroying reality] and creating a new one, that of the anal universe where *all differences are abolished.*
>
> (Chasseguet-Smirgel, 1985, p. 3, italics added)

Such conditions, she noted, result in the wholesale elimination of feelings of envy helplessness, smallness, inadequacy, absence, and fears of castration and death—every sort of psychic pain that we experience as an affront to our narcissism.

Chasseguet-Smirgel (1985) noted that anyone who considers themselves "the son of nobody" (p. 70) will, as a result, fail to introject the paternal capacities needed to creatively father a genuine piece of work based on one's link to previous generations—Sir Isaac Newton's often referenced, seventeenth-century, humble self-assessment: "If I have seen further, it is by standing on the shoulders of Giants." Another truism is the fact that parents constitute a different generation, with all that entails. Mothers who confuse their sons by treating them as surrogate husbands ("Oedipal victors")—itself an act of perversity—do them a mighty disservice, as illustrated in the life and writings of D. H. Lawrence (see Chapter 5). Another irrefutable aspect of reality is the matter of the binary existence of two types of human beings: men and women. With the rare exception of hermaphrodism, there are two, and only two, genders—male and female. Laplanche (2011a), who was otherwise critical of Stoller's thinking, nonetheless saw merit in Stoller's binary definition of core gender identity as "the belief or feeling that one belongs to one of two genders" (p. 134). The realities of birth, death, generations, and the binary nature of gender—which, granted, is presently disputed—can be considered truths with which each of us must contend. A refusal to do so debatably constitutes perversity.

The Work of Masud Khan

Khan (1979) developed a somewhat different theory, positing that "all per-versions entail a fundamental *alienation from self* in the person concerned and the attempt is to find personalization through the elaborate machinery of sexual experiences" (p. 16). He describes how the mothers of boys who go on to develop perversions *"idolize"* their sons (relate to specific, per-ceived aspects of the child): "what the mother cathects and invests in is at once something very special in him and yet *not him as a whole person"* (p. 12, italics added). Her practice of relating exclusively to this "something special" has the effect of alienating the boy from himself. The boy becomes *dissociated* from his true (authentic) self, and thereafter is incapable of "showing up" to relationships as an authentic being given the extent to which the boy identifies with this internal object—the mother's "thing-creation" (Khan, 1979, p. 12). Khan noted that he had yet to meet a pervert whose behavior was driven by "authentic instinctual pressure," noting "it is all engineered from the head" (p. 14) (involves the process of *sexualization*).

A Perspective Provided by Phyllis Greenacre

While Greenacre (2003) agrees with most authors who posit that early trauma can trigger the development of perversion, she leaves room for traumatic situations that don't involve lapses in good-enough mothering—traumas asso-ciated with a "suffusion of excitement and an overflow of discharge with premature stimulation of zonal responses for which the infant is not matur-ationally ready" (p. 104). Greenacre describes the development of *pre-Oedipal fetishes* (those *unassociated* with the sight of a penisless being) that are triggered by trauma in the first 18 months of life—instances when the use of a transitional object fails to suffice, resulting in the generation of intense aggression. She suggests such conditions don't ripen into adult fetishization unless and until the child suffers the types of *Oedipal* traumas thought to trigger the fetishization process. Whether pre-Oedipal trauma and pre-Oedi-pal fetishes are prerequisites to the development of adult fetishization is left unclear in Greenacre's thinking.

A Lacanian Perspective

At this juncture, it helps to present ideas that, at first glance, may seem tan-gential to Stoller's theories about the psychological development of the male species or those positing the origins of perversity. Notwithstanding the fact Lacanian thinking might not seem to directly bear on the subject of perver-sity, Lacan's thinking does in fact relate directly to one of this book's main topics: the psychology of the male species. For that reason, this seems a reasonable juncture to lay out what Lacan said about a man's capacity to love (see Fink, 2016).

An essential Lacanian principle posits a central aspect of the human con-dition is the fact we are all, in one way or another, simply not enough—that a sense of "lack" constitutes a core subjective experience for all humans, which helps account for the experience of desire. Lacan insisted that indivi-duals cannot account for the emptiness they feel within—simply put, they don't know what they are missing (Lacan, 2015). Lacan proposed this core sense of lack drives human behavior—in particular, a Wizard of Oz-type search to seek out what one lacks to finally feel whole and complete, be it a brain (the scarecrow), a heart (the tinman), or courage (the lion). The cliché "you complete me" illustrates a lover's declaration that he or she has found a "soulmate." Such seeking eventuates in some humans knocking on the analyst's consulting room door believing he is the one who knows and can provide what it is one lacks.

Space does not permit a full explication of Lacan's theory of lack; but it is worth mentioning in passing that this lack—which Lacan termed a *symbolic* "castration" (becoming separated from an essential aspect of oneself)—has to do with a number of matters, including our being forever severed from our unconscious, our sense of being alienated from aspects of ourself, our inability to find words that do justice to an expression of our innermost experiences (given that our language is not our own but instead is provided to us by others), to name a few. There is more to it, but let's allow this outline to suffice.

One of Lacan's more famous and confounding statements is "love is giving what you don't have" (2015, p. 129), which he elaborates by noting: "Giving what you have is throwing a party, not love" (p. 357). Rather than leave readers grasping at straws to make sense of what seems like a typical instance of Lacanian opacity, permit me to clarify. If Lacan had said "Love involves bringing to the table one's sense of insufficiency" (humbly admitting to one's lover that one is not all one wished one to be or wished one had to offer one's lover), readers would have a better sense of what he is driving at; but surely Lacan had no intention of making matters clear since he forever capitalized on the benefits of ambiguity, for better and for worse.

Bruce Fink described the consequences of a man's *inability* (refusal) to "give what he doesn't have" (to even recognize his basic lack), which appears characteristic of men who are stuck in the phallic narcissistic stage of development—those who others must suffer given their rampant toxic masculinity. He described the situation in the following fashion:

> To love someone else is to convey in words to that person that we lack—preferably big time—and that he or she is intimately related to that lack. We need not suggest that he or she fills the bill in absolutely every respect, that he or she can saturate our lack one hundred percent. But we must reveal through speech that we lack and that our lack concerns him or her.
>
> (Fink, 2016, p. 36)

To demonstrate the relevance of Lacanian thinking to male psychology requires that we follow Fink's thinking:

Men in Western culture generally seem to have a harder time than women do admitting to lack, a harder time verbally admitting that they are missing something, incomplete in some respect, limited in some way—in a word, castrated ... To love is to admit to lack ... Insofar as he is a man, he can admit to desiring the so-called partial objects he sees in his partner, but he generally feels that perfectly good partial objects of much the same kind can be found in many different partners. Insofar as he is a man, he contents himself with the enjoyment he derives from the partial objects he finds in a whole series of interchangeable partners, and avoids like the plague showing that he lacks ... to love—at least in our times—is to implicitly ask the beloved for love that can make good or somehow compensate one for one's own lack, the hollow or emptiness one feels inside.

(Fink, 2016, p. 36)

Not to be caught stereotyping, Fink (2016) elaborated upon Lacan's thinking:

Anyone, regardless of anatomy or chromosomes, who is fixated on partial objects as found in any number of fungible partners, and loath to reveal any lack, is characterized by what he calls masculine structure (akin to obsession), whereas anyone, regardless of anatomy or chromosomes, who is primarily concerned, instead, with lack and love is characterized by what he calls feminine structure. (p. 37)

Perversion defines more than just a requisite need for a fetishistic object, condition, or storyline to be present for a man to become emotionally and bodily aroused. Perversion describes more than a way of thinking (e. g., disavowal of reality) or a way of relating (e.g., sadomasochistically possessing, controlling, demeaning, or torturing another). Perversion stands in for what otherwise might have been, but—for some men—is unachievable, a relationship with someone upon whom the man might *lean*—in the "anaclitic" interpersonal sense: an object one needs given one's sense of insufficiency (lacking); an object who has something one cannot provide for oneself. A failure to lean—given the extremity of one's stereotypic belief that a man must be strong, independent, and self-sufficient—interferes with male development, resulting in a fixation at the phallic narcissistic stage of development and the development of features of toxic masculinity.

Notes

1 Another theory like Stoller's that also addresses root matters.
2 This is similar, if not equivalent, to Henri Rey's (1979, 1994) concept of the "claustro-agora-phobic dilemma." Goodman (1993) noted: "Primary anxiety thus

has two antithetical components: fear of being engulfed (claustrophobia) and fear of disintegrating ('agoraphobia'). Each represents a form of annihilation anxiety, or fear of loss of self. A complementary conflict may also be identified, between the wish for merger or fusion—in a sense, 'claustrophilia'—and the (biologically determined) drive for individuation and mastery—which can be called 'agoraphilia.' We may thus recognize a basic conflict, claustrophilia and agoraphobia versus agoraphilia and claustrophobia, which represents the first organization of conflictual forces within the psyche" (p. 96).

3   Fetishization and the Campaign to Alter Reality

Perversion in general, and the use of fetishes in particular, was originally proposed to entail the introduction of a specific item into the sexual scene to lessen the man's anxiety so that he might then be able to get erect and stay erect. Freud (1927) considered fetishism an incidental finding in the analyses of men who sought treatment for other reasons, noting such men were "quite satisfied with it [the utility of the fetish], or even praise the way in which it eases their erotic life" (p. 152). A man's need to employ fetishes reflects his inability to accept reality "as is," which requires he employ fetishization to create an illusion that things are other than they are. In the end, perversion amounts to a grand illusion.

The core Freudian concept of a fetish (Freud, 1927) sees it serving as an arousal-facilitating thing/presence that distracts the man from consciously considering an unnerving absence. Freud proposed that men who use such devices or condition are struggling with the disturbing sense, when with their sexual partner, that something is terribly amiss (something is missing), which Freud proposed to be the woman's penis—the "female phallus" young boys believe to exist, which some men, as adults, continue to need to believe to prevent an outbreak of castration anxiety that would seriously interfere with their ability to perform sexually. The calamity of the missing penis is solved with the introduction of a fetishistic object that stands in for (symbolizes) that which is missing—for example, a cigarette dangling form a woman's lips that is used to represent the penis.

By dint of the introduction of a fetish, what had gone missing is missing no more; or, more to the point, is *missing and not missing all at the same time*. Freud (1927) noted: "the fetish is a substitute for the woman's (mother's) penis that the little boy once believed in and—for reasons familiar to us— does not want to give up" (pp. 152–153). The upshot of such reasoning leads to the conclusion that the boy refuses to acknowledge the fact women lack penises, a realization some men set out to correct by altering reality so that it is more to their liking, using a fetish to that end. The danger of castration is an affront to the boy's narcissism—a situation that is mitigated with the aid of a fetish that perpetuates the childhood belief in the female phallus.

DOI: 10.4324/9781003609339-3

Beyond penislessness, which unnerves many a man, lies other challenging aspects of reality, which makes any attempt to obliterate such realities acts of perversity. Our very existence is born of the efforts of others, we did not self-generate, we are someone else's idea; and—as much as we do not like the idea—we are destined to die. Some perverse individuals are dedicated to denying these aspects of reality. Accordingly, perversion entails an alteration in one's perception of reality (Arlow 1971; Grossman, 1993; Ruszczynski, 2018), starting with the sleight-of-hand trick of turning someone lacking a penis into something who has one. The term "to pervert" describes processes that falsify, garble, distort, mistake, dissemble, obscure, and so on and so forth. In perversion, a problematic bit of reality one aims to address does not get repressed; rather, it is "disavowed" (a vertical rather than a horizontal split). "We would now say that what is perverted is knowledge of reality, both internal and external," noted Ruszczynski (2018, p. 27). "Clinical perversion may therefore be understood as fundamentally defensive, achieved primarily by deception and disavowal of reality, with the purpose of fending off unbearable affects that would otherwise have to be known and experienced" (p. 32).

Beyond Mere Castration Anxiety

Freud's theory that a fetish is a stand-in for the missing female phallus seems to adequately account for certain instances when fetishes are employed; but there are times when a fetish seems not to serve that specific aim. I am not proposing Freud's theory is wrong; rather, I am suggesting it has its limitations and must be expanded to include other types of behaviors that we now subsume under the categories "perversion" and "fetishization." This was a point Robert Stoller strove to make.

Consider, for example, an instance when a young man gets excited handling and smelling the underwear of another boy that he surreptitiously procured—perhaps retrieving it from the dirty laundry pile. The young man masturbates using that fetish, which serves as a *stand-in* for the boy whose penis had been in close physical proximity with the undergarment. The masturbator feels sexually attracted to the boy but hasn't the nerve to make a move to initiate a potential sexual event; so he does what he considers the next best thing: he creates an illusion that the boy is in fact present, truth to the contrary. In this fashion, the fetish creates an illusion, and by doing so plays with reality—but not in the service of managing castration anxiety per se.

Another illustration of a case in which a fetishistic object was used to achieve a different sort of psychological aim is presented by Margaret Rubin (2025) in her paper on a middle-aged, celibate married man whose secret and sole sexual object was a collection of male chastity belts he interchangeably used on a regular basis to arouse himself sexually—a practice that led to his losing himself in time. He noted that these form-fitting belts—which numbered over 200—felt to him like a "second skin." They provided him with a sense of containment, safety, and security—a reassuring feeling that "he was intact and safe from his tormentors." The belts provided him with a method of *self*-arousal (eschewing experiencing himself being aroused by other autonomous beings). He used these restraints to hold back sexual release, sustaining tumescence for hours on end; the longer he remained restrained, the greater his ultimate orgasm. The pornography he watched predictably involved men and women in restraints, sex slaves, and medieval torture devices. This man was self-contained—he was at the same time both his own dominatrix and a sex slave. He needed no one else; he could do it all himself.

The patient's childhood was calamitous and grim: a distant father prone to physical violence; a mother who walked about naked, emotionally disengaged, "a breeze he could never touch." The patient was a loner and spoke of living "in a universe of one," feeling like "a nothing," living a life of fantasy. His mother was so maternally ill-equipped that she was completely incapable of caring for him or—for that matter—for herself, resulting in his becoming the mother's parent-like caretaker.

Many factors contributed to the creation of this fetishistic practice, chief amongst which was the mother's practice, when the patient was four years old, of harnessing him on a leash and walking him around the neighborhood as one might a dog—an experience the patient loved insofar as it involved a type of physical contact that excited him to no end. When he was six years old, he tied himself up with a jump rope and found it made him feel safe and contained. When he was 11 years old, he used a bicycle chain as a restraint, leading him to orgasm. During adolescence, he would swaddle himself with the aid of restraints to calm himself down and manage an upsurge of murderous rage and sexual arousal.

Clinical evidence strongly suggested the patient experienced himself and his mother as one and the same. Sometimes he had the uncanny feeling they shared the same mind. He spoke of how his mother's "skeletal system" lived within him—hinting at an ongoing state of desired/feared merger with the woman he described as a "barnacle." One dream fragment pictured him and his naked mother entangled in a medieval restraint, a horrifying image forever linking them in his unconscious.

Once in restraints, the patient would don lace panties over the belt that reminded him of something his mother would wear. To this he then added two women's bathing suit bottoms and, finally, a pair of his boxer shorts. The belt served both to protect him against castration and to cause his own castration as far as he often felt genderless when restrained. Many of the patient's dreams pictured him as a woman. The dream that ushered in his abandoning his fetishistic practice was one in which "I could feel my musculature separate from my skeletal system." During the following day's analytic session, the patient noted: "I think I need to stop using the belt. It's my mother's skeletal system after all."

This man's use of such fetishes appeared to sustain an illusion that he and his mother were one, which denied the reality that he and she were not only separate beings but beings further separated by dint of differences in their bodies—a reality that, if acknowledged, would burn the bridge behind him, making complete reunion with her impossible. This harkens back to Stoller's emphasis on how the boy's separation/individuation from mother comes at a terrible psychic cost, which the boy, on his way to manhood, must find ways to manage or solve. It also touches on Mervin Glasser's idea that perversion often involves a striving to merge with a mother/mother figure.

These two clinical presentations of fetishistic practices illustrate the point Bach (1991) made when he wrote: "from a certain perspective, one might say that a person has a perversion instead of a relationship" (p. 75). While these cases illustrate Bach's point to a tee, the degree to which fetishization interferes with interpersonal relations should be considered to exist on a continuum, as will be illustrated in the next section.

Intolerance of the Raw Reality of Another Being

Fetishization involves refashioning reality to make it more psychically tolerable. Fetishization is not limited to the use of substitute objects (things), it can also involve an alteration of one's perception of others. Certain men cannot tolerate the raw reality of another's being, that person's defining subjectivity, so they objectify or fetishize them, making them seem to be other than who they are, accomplished by ignoring aspects that make them whole, complete objects. Fetishization can help make one's involvement with another more tolerable by diluting one's experience and awareness of the fullness of the other's being, accomplished either by inserting something *between* self and other (such as a fantasy), or by focusing on a select body part.

During a sexual encounter with a given woman, a man closes his eyes and imagines (inserts an image of) himself making love to another woman. By doing so, the man successfully dilutes the intensity of the here-and-now encounter he is having with the woman he presently is with. Fetishization can also involve substituting a *part* of another (e.g., a physical part: the woman's breasts, her behind) in place of experiencing the entirety of the woman—the fullness of her being. This also functions as a classic fetish to the extent the man's attention is diverted from attending to some intolerable aspect of her being.

Some men are attracted to a "type" of woman—for example, redheads, waif-like women, passive women, ballsy women, and so on and so forth. Focusing narrowly on a particular physical attribute or character trait also represents a form of fetishization to the extent the woman becomes objectified and one-dimensionalized, which dispenses with the *defining particulars of her being* in the process. A "piece" of the woman is highlighted, which then becomes her sole defining feature, turning her into a generic class of women (e.g., redheads), thus robbing her of what the man experiences as her dangerous uniqueness. Such processes are dehumanizing, which Cooper (1991) refers to as "the ultimate strategy against the *fears of human qualities*—it protects against the vulnerability of loving, against the possibility of human unpredictability, and against the sense of power- lessness and passivity in comparison to other humans" (pp. 23–24, italics added).

The perverse individual's campaign to alter reality includes imaging others and treating others as pawns to be moved about on the chessboard of one's mind, often with the aid of fantasies that perverts the realities of the other. Dehu- manization involves stripping others of their personal attributes, which interferes with the perverse individual's wish to use them as he sees fit—specifically, to enlist them in the enactment of his perverse fantasy. De Masi (1999, p. 79) described just how perverse individuals alter the reality of the people in their lives or those they encounter when out and about:

> Objects live only to the extent that they perform the tasks assigned to them by the imagination. If the partner were experienced as alive and independent, the freedom and omnipotence of fantasy could not exist; a real partner with his or her own requirements or needs sets a limit to the imagination and, as such, diminishes the level of excitation.

Character Perversion

Beyond the use of a fetish to make something that is absent appear present; beyond perverse modes of thinking that, like a pea-under-the-shell game, rearrange reality to suit the perverse individual's needs; beyond perverse modes of relating that treat others as part objects is a more pervasive form of perversion that is to as a "character perversion" (Arlow, 1971; Grossman, 1992, 1993). Such perversity involves imposing one's fantasies on others, enlisting them to play a part in the enactment of one's perverse fantasy, the imposition of which is a *further* act of perversity. McDougall (1995) sur- mised: "Perhaps in the last resort, only relationships can aptly be termed perverse; this label would then apply to sexual exchanges in which the per- verse individual is totally indifferent to the needs and desires of the other" (pp. 177–178).

The more that pathological narcissism (versus neurotic mechanisms) con- tributes to the creation of a perversion (Kernberg, 1992), the more the per- version will serve to defend against psychotic anxieties (Glover, 1933; Malcolm, 1970; Stein, 2005), ward off disintegration (Goldberg, 1995), or relieve a sense of deadness (Khan, 1979). Under such conditions, one sees a heightened tendency to disavow reality, to refashion it into something the individual can better tolerate, which reflects a significant impairment in the individual's grasp of reality (Arlow, 1971; Chasseguet-Smirgel, 1981, 1985, 1991; Grossman, 1992, 1993, 1996; Jimenez, 2004; Zimmer 2003).

Fantasy as Fetish

The degree to which fantasy becomes a lover's primary preoccupation is a measure of the extent to which that fantasy functions as a fetish that, like all fetishes, helps facilitate the disavowal of some anxiety-arousing bit of reality that inhibits the man's sexual arousal. Sexual fantasies of the sort Stoller described can be just as effective at quelling anxiety as standard fetishistic objects (e.g., stiletto heels), which help divert the man's attention away from his sexual partner's penisless state and on to the fetish that is chosen as a stand-in for what otherwise would be recognized as missing (Freud, 1927).

In the case of the fetishistic use of fantasy, the unbearable reality that must be disavowed is the raw, subjective presence of another that demands to be recognized for who that person is and for what that person desires. Khan's (1979) concept of the etiology of perversion was based on a belief that perversion was born of a man's experience with his mother who would not or could not see him for who he was and, instead, related to him as if he was everything she wanted and needed him to be. A man's over-reliance on a fetish can be thought to turn a supposedly interactive sexual scene into something more akin to masturbation. Tausk (1951, p. 61) notes:

> The criterion which determines whether a sexual act is either a masturbatory one or intercourse is not given in the external form of the sexual behavior but in the psychic superstructure of the physical process ... Many a man will confess that he masturbates with his penis in the vagina of a woman.

The extent to which one's fantasies dictate not only the specific nature of what must, and must not, take place during a sexual encounter but also who the lover can and cannot be is a measure of the degree to which that fantasy functions like any other fetish, serving to lessen anxiety. This is particularly true of men, who are considerably more prone to fetishize their sexual objects in comparison to women.

The extent to which one's fantasies monopolize one's sexual life varies from man to man. Some men end up glued to their computer screens, surfing the internet in search of a kaleidoscope of images that correspond to their preferred fantasies. These men oftentimes find that sexual encounters with real women pale by comparison, to the extent no woman can hope to identically replicate the man's fantasy; furthermore, women often and—complicating matters— many women expect their sexual partners to make room for a consideration of their fantasies and desires. While fantasy may underlie every man's sexual life, it does so to varying degrees. Times when fantasy plays a dominant role are times when it is likely to function as a fetish, with all the limitations that typically places on the breadth of the man's sexual life.

Oftentimes, fantasies of who we need the other to be seriously limit our ability to recognize others for who they are. Between the extremes of intimacy and perversity, some men can see their object more clearly for who they are than other men can. Intimacy is reflected in one's capacity to "bear the brunt of one another's subjectivity... as providing (or sustaining the) proof of one another's existence" (Cavell, 1988, p. 91), in contrast with men who lose sight of the other in favor of their preferred fantasy, a practice that is fetishistic in that a "thing"—in this case, a fantasy—becomes inserted into what would otherwise be the raw experiencing of the other. Kirshner (2005) sums this up by noting how

> The lover must accept that his or her passionate fantasies are inventions that even when apparently reciprocated *do not erase the gap between one's private feelings and the reality of the other*. We might even pro-pose that acknowledgment of this discrepancy—that one's beloved is other than the fantasy or subjective object ...—is a necessary step for symbolic love to proceed. (pp. 86–87, italics added)

Some men are "obligatory" fetishists in that they can *only* have sex if parti-cular conditions are met, while others—quite capable of becoming "turned on" by a wide variety of attractive women—nevertheless hold out for a woman who is their "type" (e.g., a redhead). Taken to extremes, the pursuit of one's "type" can lead to a man who dates and marries a succession of women, all of whom bear a striking and creepy resemblance to one another.[1] Taking up the issue of a man having a "type," Balint (1956, p. 20) wonders:

> Is it normal or not to demand that the love object must be tall or petite, fair or dark, very bright, or rather simple, domineering, or submissive, and so on? Perhaps we may accept the conditions just quoted as normal; [but] when they exact that a woman limp or even have a false leg ... that the woman wear black underwear during coitus, the difficulty of drawing a boundary becomes greater.

Balint raises a critical question: Can both ends of the spectrum be considered fetishistic without stretching the term to the point of meaningless—to the point it ceases to draw any clear distinction? What does *preferring* redheads say about a man, and is such a man quantitatively or qualitatively different from one who *requires* his lover have red hair before he can even conceive of having sex with her?

When an individual feels it necessary to require other human beings to play a role in the enactment of his fantasy, perversity rises to another level. This is less concerning when the man's sexual partner freely agrees to play a role in accordance with the man's fantasy (when it suits her needs as well or, at least, is not a "turn-off" to her); but instances when the fantasizer enlists the unwitting help of a stranger are more deeply troubling—instances when perversity is defined by more than the content of the story as it comes to represent a *perverse mode of relating to others* (Bach, 1991; Filippini, 2005; Stein, 2005; Tuch, 2008, 2010). Involving others in an enactment of one's own fantasy at the other's expense—forcing them into an enactment without their say-so or their sense of what comes next—is deeply disturbed and disturbing not just to the victim but to society in general, as we shall see in Chapter 8, which takes up the phenomenon of genital exhibitionism.

Note

1 Here, we can wonder whether the term "creepy" perfectly describes the perverse act.

4 Male Pride, Men's Dread of Women, and the Effort to Neutralize Female Power

Male and female psychologies diverge in a host of ways, beginning with differences in the durability of men's and women's respective senses of gender identity—the degree to which each gender can sustain an unwavering sense of themselves as masculine or feminine (as opposed to male vs. female, *core* gender identity). In comparison to women, who have an easier time maintaining a sense of themselves as feminine, men collectively experience a sense of their masculinity as relatively fragile, given that it can, and often is, subtly and not so subtly called into question by others and by the man himself. Such conditions leave men needing, for example, to persistently attend to how they are acting to ensure they do not give others the wrong impression by appearing less than solidly and unequivocally masculine.

Some might argue the pressure to conform to societal pressures is a thing of the past given cultural shifts in how masculinity is defined and gets decided. While this is true to some extent, it is hard to believe the collective durability of men's sense of masculinity has suddenly firmed to such an extent that many men no longer feel challenged when their masculinity is questioned. It is, after all, typical—particularly when it comes to toxically masculine men, to make locker-room type sport of other men, shaming them by suggesting they are something less than men.

Evidence of cultural shifts in the sorts of behaviors that had once been deemed—in a regrettable and pejorative use of the term, "gay" (excusing me for saying)—is provided by the 2007 movie *Superbad*, starring Jonah Hill as Seth and Michael Cera as Evan, close childhood friends who are now high school seniors. Long ago they had made a pact that they would not part ways and would attend the same college after graduation; but this is not how things are playing out. Seth is hurt when Evan decides to attend Dartmouth, a school that lies beyond Seth's reach. Seth confronts Evan, angrily accusing him of "bailing" on their agreement. Evan fires back, accusing Seth of being selfish, adding that he is sick and tired of feeling "held back" by Evan. Though both characters are unquestionably straight, the audience has the impression they are watching a lovers' spat. Making matters worse, Seth overhears a mutual friend (nicknamed "McLovin") mention that he and Evan

DOI: 10.4324/9781003609339-4

plan to room together at Dartmouth—adding the element of exclusion and jealousy to Evan's palpable sense of abandonment.

Seth and Evan have a sleepover. They are lying on the ground in sleeping bags situated in close proximity. They begin to talk in hushed tones about matters that seem decidedly unmasculine if measured by the conventional standards of yesteryear. Seth admits to having feelings he had been holding in. He tells Evan he felt jealous when he learned, weeks before, that Evan would be rooming with McLovin. Seth responds in a sensitive fashion. He takes the opportunity to reassure Seth by sharing the fact he is not enamored with the idea of rooming with McLovin, and is only doing so because he fears rooming with a stranger.

Such emotionally frank discussions picturing two boys who clearly feel emotionally close to one another, two boys who aren't afraid to "open up" to each other by sharing intimate details of their attachment to one another, is a testament to how far things have come in our culture's acceptance of such expressions of male–male tenderness, which need not call into question either boy's degree of masculinity. While courage to speak openly about one's feelings can arguably be considered a present-day mertric of masculinity, and while it is heartening to see portrayals of male–male intimacy that reflect an enlightened sense of what it means to be a man, in my estimation such changes don't yet (and may never) constitute the norm, making the defense of one's right to claim to be a man a matter with which men will continue to struggle.

Claiming one's right to be considered sufficiently masculine leads to the topic of what colloquially is referred to as "male ego"—the term "ego" being used in the lay sense of the term (pride or narcissism) and not in the way psychoanalysts use it. The phallic phase of development is characterized by just such "phallic pride"—a boy's pride in being duly equipped with a magnificent organ that can perform amazing, awe-inspiring feats. At this point, women might feel a bit nauseated reading such an egotistical description of how men think, but I won't let that deter me from making such observations explicit. I am not defending; I am only reporting.

It is worth nothing that many wise women wishing to maintain harmonious relationships with members of the opposite sex often take care—without taking undo umbrage—not to trample on a man's pride, though most women make sure not to bend over backwards doing so since such back-breaking efforts often come at a cost. Acknowledging "penis envy" as a reality can be a woman's way of supporting a man's proud investment in his prized member. Men owe women a debt of gratitude for the favor of supporting their pride, though only a select few might willingly admit as much—particularly men who would consider such an acknowledgment less than manly.

So, what about male pride? Don't women have comparable issues with pride? The simple answer is "yes" and "no." Women have challenges of their own, but fighting to prove themselves sufficiently feminine is not high on the list of things that occupy women's minds.[1] Male pride—a pride in being able to lay claim to being a man—is more fragile than is a woman's sense of her womanliness. Like the question of paternity, one's sense of manliness is always at risk; it can and does intermittently get challenged under certain conditions, sometimes taking place between the sheets, other times taking place on the metaphoric battlefield where men challenge one another, time and again, to prove themselves worthy of being considered masculine.

Strutting about in peacock-like fashion risks the chance of getting cut down to size. Alpha males who are out to stake their claim leave other men no option but to bow in accordance or stand ready to challenge the hierarchical order. Here, we are not far from our primate relatives, save for the fact humans have an expanded way of displaying masculinity. A man can make up for his lack of brawn by displaying his braininess: his cleverness, sense of humor, unflappable demeanor, talented tongue—all signs of mental agility that help establish the man's mating value through displays of attributes that establish him as being sufficiently masculine to woo and win a woman's hand. Beyond such obvious mating displays, a man must remain perpetually on guard against the ever-present danger of being regarded, for whatever reason, as less than a man—as castrated, as womanly, as cuckold.

Potential injury to a man's pride issues from many different sources. Men are expected to gather their courage and pursue women despite the fear of rejection or the imagined prospect of having their sexual performance judged as less than impressive. A mating display of self-confidence is something women find attractive—it demonstrates the man has "the balls" to stick out his neck and let his desire be known. Once he has won the woman over, the man must show he can get erect (a sticking point for some) and stay erect (a sticking point for others), not cum too quickly (a third hurdle to jump), He must also demonstrate his ("know-how") as well as the wherewithal to pleasure a woman several times over. For some men, this is a tall order. Anxiety or a lack of self-confidence can screw things up at any point along the way, which further contributes to the fragility of a man's sense of masculinity.

To this day—despite enlightened thinking about gender roles that one might think would put such concerns to rest—men expect themselves (and believe women likewise expect them) to demonstrate sufficient strength to make the woman feel the man is someone on whom she can lean on and depend. A man's capacity to express hurt, insecurity, or sensitivity can cause some women to worry that the man will not be the Rock of Gibraltar she needs him to be. A man who can cry—a man unthreatened by emotionality—might strike some women as attractive, but only to a certain degree. Excessive emotionality is a mixed bag. If a man's emotionality is excessive, a woman is left to wonder whether he could serve as a port in a storm. As for "house husbands," I would like to believe we have evolved to the point that a husband's earning capacity is not a factor in the couple's dynamic;

however, I have trouble finding sufficient evidence to back the claim, and know of many instances when a disparity between the earning capacities of husband and wife becomes a major issue in the relationship. I mention this not to endorse such beliefs, only to catalog them for the reader's consideration.

Central to the issue of male pride is a man's comfort allowing himself to admit to needing a woman; his capacity to feel comfortable turning to and relying on others—to be able to need a woman but to not need her to an excessive degree. Concerns about the implication of needing a woman date back to a time when the boy was developmentally required to relinquish his "leaning on" (anaclitic) tendencies that had characterized his earliest relationship with the mother. If admitting one *needs* a woman leads a man (or the woman in his life) to believe he is being "*needy,*" one is confronted with a problem some men (and couples)—perhaps many—must face. There is, after all, nothing attractive about a "needy" man, which leads some men to engage in self-deception to keep their needs from emerging. Such matters lie at the heart of male psychology. There is an excess of "unavailable men" ("avoidant" style of attachment) relative to "unavailable women," which speaks volumes. The Eagles song "Desperado"—which tells the tale of a man who seeks independence but learns such yearnings can imprison him, keeping him from the rewards of human involvement—would never work as a song about a woman.

A man's sense of masculinity can be challenged on two fronts—by other men and by the women in their lives. Many men are unsettled by the degree to which they feel their sense of self-worth as a man lies chiefly in the hands of the woman they desire—a situation that contributes to men's dread of women, a concept brought to light nearly a century ago by renegade psychoanalyst Karen Horney (1932), whose essays helped launch the feminist movement of the 1970s. Horney found evidence, in the treatments she conducted, to support her claim that men recognize and fear the power women hold over their sense of self-worth, that men experience women as a "menace" to their ability to feel a reasonable modicum of "self-respect" as a sexual being.

Validation for Horney's theory is easy to find. Consider, for example, the biblical tale of Delilah, who, like Eve, got a man into a heap of trouble. Delilah double-crossed Samson twice. First, she goaded him to reveal the secret source of his physical strength, arguing that if he truly loved her he would confide in her; then, after Samson took the bait and divulged the source of his power was his hair, Delilah betrayed him again by shaving his head, turning him into a shell of the man he had once been. The moral of the story: Men beware, you have cause for concern. The Islamic practice of requiring women to wear a burka, purportedly for the sake of modesty, turns the tables. Now, the woman is shorn of her advantage over men—her Siren-like ability to weaken men by her sheer physical attractiveness; or, in the case of the myth of the Sirens, the fatal allure of her singing.

The Perverse (Fetishistic) Nature of Male Sexual Fantasy

Male fantasies tend to objectify (fetishize) women in comparison to women's fantasies about men. The same is true of the pornography men watch, which often portrays storylines involving power and domination over women, additional forms of fetishization. One notable difference between what interests men versus women is the female preference for romance-based pornography, which does not appear on lists of the types of porn men enjoy watching. Rather, male fantasies and preferred pornography tend to be more visually oriented and body-part focused, hence more fetishistic in nature.

For some men, the comfort of watching their preferred fantasy play out on screen feels safer and more satisfying than having to contend with the risks associated with engaging sexually with a real human being who has wishes and desires of her own—a woman who requires the man to perform, exposing him to the ego-threatening peril of being judged insufficient. Porn is advantageous to the extent it provides the man a chance to see his favored fantasy play out to a tee in accordance with his given proclivity without having to worry about pleasing his sexual partner or being judged by her.

Stoller argued that the meaning of a sexual act, what made it exciting, did not depend so much on whom one is "doing," nor what the two are doing, rather, it's all about the backstory that lends the action meaning in the minds of those involved, which brings us back to the topic of erotic plots or storylines. Picture, if you will, a man getting a blowjob. What exactly is happening here? Perhaps he is imagining the woman is being forced by him to have to submit and, in the process, is being both dominated and demeaned (e.g., "on your knees, b**ch").[2] That is one way the story can be told. How else might the action be thought to mean? Perhaps the woman's skill in giving blowjobs is beyond anything the man had ever experienced. She is pictured, in the man's mind, as being in complete control of his pleasure. She dominates; he is submitting to her prowess and power, and is loving every bit of it—not just because it feels good, but perhaps because *the story he is telling himself satisfies his wish to submit*. Stoller emphasized time and again the importance of the story one tells oneself, which makes all the difference in the world as to whether something is or is not sexually arousing.

Domination and submission (do or be done to) are like yin and yang—they are part and parcel of the whole. Freud was clear about the matter. A man alternately might wish to dominate or to be dominated—which of the two he prefers speaks volumes about his psychology. Some perverse fantasies explicitly tell a tale of a man's domination over women, while others picture the man submitting masochistically to the woman who appears to be dominating him. If one reads between the lines of such supposedly masochistic fantasy/acts, one finds evidence that the supposed act of submission involves the masochist covertly enlisting the sadist to do his bidding, all the while making it appear otherwise, bracketing his desire. Stoller notes such masochistic fantasies represent a victory of sorts. The man *actively authored* the fantasy/enactment: No one made him dream it up; no one forced him to seek it out—it was of his doing. Furthermore, by enduring and surviving the imagined or enacted torture—by not having been defeated or destroyed by what was done to him (in fantasy or reality)—the man rises like a phoenix from the ashes. Others had tried, but failed, to cut him down to size. Such reasoning lies at the heart of Stoller's thinking about the traumatic roots of perversion.

A careful reading of Stoller indicates he thought all men, at their core, exhibit perverse tendencies. Rather than consider perversity to be an all-or-nothing matter, I believe it makes more sense to think in terms of *degrees* of perversity, seeing it as a spectrum phenomenon. The degree of perversity might then be measured by how mandatory it feels to the man to rectify his childhood traumas by harming, controlling, or demeaning others, in fantasy or reality, who serves as stand-ins for the original tormentor. The more necessary such rectifying efforts are experienced as being—the more time and energy spent thinking about the story or watching it play out on screen—the more perverse we would consider the man to be given his *degree of engagement*—the extent to which his perverse fantasies have taken hold of him. The more "space" such fantasies occupy in one's mind, the more time spent searching the internet for just the right porn that will hit the spot, the more psychologically impairing the fantasy will prove to be. Countless hours, which could be better spent, before a screen in endless pursuit of a storyline that closely approximates his gratifying fantasies, the more impaired we would judge that man to be seeing how fleeting such seeming solutions are known to be. The same is true of inverse types of fantasies that picture the man on the receiving end of abusive treatment.

We call fantasies or enacted fantasies perverse if they objectify or dehumanize ("fetishize") another human being or they represent a hostile attempt to put down, demean, denigrate, debase, humiliate, defile, disempower, discredit, damage, diminish, or in whatever imaginable ways harm the other. "The study of perversion," Stoller (1974b) concluded, "is the study of hostility more than of libido" (p. 429)—a perspective that challenges our thinking about male sexual fantasy.

Stoller theorized that the source of sexual fantasies, or "erotic daydreams," emanates from various childhood traumas, which include: 1) being belittled, demeaned, or humiliated by those upon whom one had depended; 2) being overly stimulated by adult caregivers when young—forced to cope with an unbearable degree of arousal, as happens when a mother routinely exposes her son to her naked body or a man inducts a prepubescent boy into the sexual world by giving him an unwelcomed and unrequested blowjob, overwhelming the boy with feelings of excitement, confusion, and shame; 3) having one's impulses held in check by a caregiver who threatens to inflict bodily harm should the child persist in engaging in forbidden behaviors, as Little Hans' mother threatened to do (e.g., "you keep playing with your pecker and I'll cut it off!"). While many might assume such occurrences are the exception, Stoller believed they were more commonplace than many imagined.

Stoller asserted such childhood traumas trigger anger and hostility, feelings with which the developing boy must contend in whatever way he can—fantasy, in Stoller's opinion, being the chief method. Stoller considered some (most? all?) male erotic daydreams/fantasies perverse.[3] Surely, some are—particularly those an individual tries to actualize by acting them out with another living being. We will leave open the question of whether all male sexual fantasies are perverse.

Stoller suggested that the traumatized child thirsts for revenge; he imagines triumphantly turning the tables on the one who had done him wrong. The growing boy or the grown man tells himself a story, a daydream, which pictures him in the driver's seat—the one calling the shots, the big shot who cannot and will not be pushed around. Now, the shoe is on the other foot. Fantasies function in this way to redress the original power imbalance that had left the boy feeling overpowered, outmaneuvered, frightened, vulnerable, and humiliated. Fantasy places the once victimized individual in a position to henceforth victimize others—to entice, frighten, shame, and frustrate them to avenge his original mistreatment, which serves both as retribution and an attempt at restitution. The fantasizing individual gets back at his victimizer using present-day people—imagined or real—as proxies to right a wrong: "First, you did it to me. Now, I do it back to you with the aid of a stand-in (via proxy). Now, we are even." But the fantasy—whether used for self-stimulation or acted out with others—never quite does the trick, which means it must be repeated endlessly, adding an element of compulsivity to the fantasy. This is the essence of Stoller's theory of perverse fantasy. Whether it accounts universally for all sexual fantasies is debatable, but there is ample evidence to suggest it accounts for certain instances of fantasy.

An example of such table-turning is illustrated by an instance of a young boy who had felt intensely anxious having to endure the sight of his sister and mother nakedly prancing about the house with their genitals on full display (Arlow, 1971). The boy fashioned an ingenious method of fighting back, which represented the actualization of vengeful fantasy. He artfully wrapped a small piece of black paper around three of his top front teeth, effectively creating the illusion of toothlessness, and nonchalantly went about his business.[4] When his mother noticed his "toothlessness" she was aghast, which filled the boy with glee having caught his mother in a "gotcha" moment indicative of the goal of practical jokers (a form of perversity). The boy removed the paper, demonstrating the whole affair had been a hoax. The hoax turned the tables in an act of revenge—sadistically creating in the mother feelings she had previously aroused in him.

The Unique Aspect of Male Sexual Fantasy

The topic of sexual daydreams leads to a brief discussion of pornography—a topic discussed at greater length in Chapter 7. Everyone has their own semi-unique sexual fantasies, and those fantasies determine the individual's taste for a specific genre of pornography. One watches the type of porn that most closely approximates what one is prone to imagine for the purpose of self-stimulation and masturbation. The type of pornography I am referring to features a well-developed storyline—Stoller (2009) calls them "erotic plots"—which is an essential part of what makes the porn exciting beyond naked bodies doing whatever with whomever.

Stoller noted that fantasy and pornography entail an element of objec-tification. When a man objectifies his sexual partner, he sees her as being none other than who he thinks her to be. This is how perversion in general, and fetishization, in particular, succeeds at altering one's sense of reality. Such conditions seriously restrict the objectified party from being able to outgrow the restraints of being specifically defined so as to be able to come into her own. The woman must swim upstream to express her authenticity; the man must grapple with the task of figuring out his partner's true identity.

There is a world of difference between the types of sexual fantasies men have relative to women. Men's fantasies tend to operate fetishistically, meaning they picture women being treated as objects to do with as he pleases. When fantasy operates in the context of being with another human being it effectively keeps the man from having to come into close contact with the true nature of who that person is, her identity. The fetishistic use of fantasy keeps the man from having to come into close contact with the full-ness of the woman's being. The fetish/fantasy keeps the woman close, but not dangerously so. Karen Horney suggested that men dread women, but not to such a degree that they want nothing to do with them. Men deal with women's dangerous allure—like the Greek myth of the Sirens whose songs induced sailors to throw themselves overboard to their deaths—by meta-phorically tying themselves to the mast. They institute measures that lessen what they fear to be the woman's threatening potential to reel them in and possess them, threatening the man's dignity and his sense of autonomy and agency.

Sexual fantasy differs in an important respect from what happens when two consenting adults, each relating (as much as they can tolerate) to the otherness of the other, get between the sheets and do their thing, whatever that might be. A sexual fantasy is a sexual scene conjured up in an indivi-dual's mind that pictures something one is *doing to* another, something *being done to* one by another—note the difference—or things one is doing *with*, not *to*, another. "Done to" versus "done with" captures the essence of fetishization.

Sexual fantasy, particularly when it becomes manifest on screen, typically extends beyond the bounds of what reality can offer, which is not to say men do not seek and sometimes find real-life situations that come close to approximating their fantasies. When it comes to pornography, a man need not contend with the "taste and smell of a living and breathing being" (quoting here from the movie *Don Jon,* to be described further along in Chapter 7)—that is, with the particulars of the woman's personhood that might mess with the purity of a man's fantasy. If a man aspires to form a deep and lasting bond with another, he must make room for a consideration of who his lover is beyond who he imagines, expects, or requires her to be, the epitome of his fantasy.

A meaningful sexual encounter, one that is not masturbatory, takes into consideration what excites one's sexual partner rather than assuming she is a double for what the man had seen portrayed on the screen: a women whose inner life is irrelevant, a woman who exists solely for the purpose of satisfying the man's desires, a woman with no desires of her own or, at least, none that require something from the man that lies outside the bounds of his fantasy life.

Some men act as if they expect and require their lovers to sexually respond in ways that reinforce their egoistic self-image that imagines themselves to be men capable of delighting women with their sexual prowess— men with expertise, men who know precisely how to turn women on. By contrast, meaningful sexual encounters require a man to learn a thing or two from his partner about what excites her rather than merely assuming all women are alike. This requirement potentially introduces an element of anxiety into the sexual act. Suddenly the quality of the man's performance is on the line, being put to the test, which had not been the case either in his fantasy life or in the porn he watches. This detail distinguishes fantasy from reality and explains a bit about why men insist that pornography and actual sexual encounters have little to do with one another.

Sexual fantasies that picture a woman in a weak or compromised position vis-a-vis the man is one way a man can manage his dread of woman and the feeling he is at her mercy in that she can choose whether to accept his invitation or satisfy his stated desire. Men who like to imagine they are in control can picture it thus in their fantasies and in the porn they watch. The story lines that play out as one watches naked bodies in action intensifies the sexual arousal and sexual satisfaction that comes from masturbating as one imagines one's favorite fantasy or watches one's favored brand of pornography.

Notes

1 However, women might compete for a given man's attention, as showcased in such reality shows as *The Bachelor,* which creates conditions conducive to showing off just such tendencies.

2 My apologies for framing it this fashion; but doing so captures how some men think and feel, so I feel obliged to represent such attitudes to the best of my ability.
3 Stoller (1975) hints at the possibility all sexual fantasies are perverse in his book on perversion, where he writes: "perhaps for every person there is *the* sexual fantasy (? perversion)" (p. 115).
4 Here, a psychoanalyst would equate the appearance of toothlessness with the boy's view of his sister and mother as penisless.

5   Sons and Mothers

D. H. Lawrence's Treatise on Male Psychology

The developmental theory Robert Stoller offers to account for the path by which boys acquire a sense of themselves as masculine beings (movement from merger to autonomy) and the one Mervin Glasser offers to account for perversity (the regressive pull from autonomy to merger) are skeletal, theoretical constructs that require some flesh be applied to the bone—some clinical material or something approximating clinical material that might help substantiate what these theorists claim to be the case. Such material is found in the work of D. H. Lawrence. After reading two of his semi-autobiographical novels—*Sons and Lovers* (1913) and *Women in Love* (1920)—along with a slew of letters and essays he wrote describing his relationship with his mother, one gets a sense of how much his fear of the danger of merger played in his ability to become and remain his own person in the face of regressive trends set in motion when he tried to forge a loving relation with a woman who, at some level, brings mother to mind.

In its day, *Women in Love* was a sexually daring novel published in an era that benefited from the liberating effect Freudian thinking was having on notions about what might be allowed to appear in print. Notwithstanding, the book's prequel—*The Rainbow* (1915)—was banned after being judicially ruled obscene, resulting in the seizure and burning of as many copies of the book as could be found, which delayed publication of *Women in Love* for several years. That novel, heralded as a masterpiece, is widely recognized as a significant piece of twentieth-century literature, reflected in its inclusion in Harold Bloom's book *The Western Canon* (1994).

One of the more remarkable aspects of *Women in Love* is the book's exploration of the psychology of its main male characters—Rupert Birkin and Gerald Crich. Lawrence's focus on male psychology makes the novel's title—*Women in Love*—curious. The book describes two types of men, each of whom grapples with the challenge of finding it within him to love the woman he fancies. Rupert and Gerald are two brands of man, which Lawrence effectively juxtaposes without implying they represent the universe of men. Their respective love interests are the Brangwen sisters (the women who supposedly are in love): Ursula, whom Rupert pursues, and Gudrun, upon whom Gerald has set his sights.

DOI: 10.4324/9781003609339-5

Rupert and Gerald differ in one important respect: Lawrence, in the guise of Rupert, is fed up with being mothered; he has had his fill, and then some. Gerald, on the other hand, yearns to be mothered, having received so little of it from his own mother. Lawrence describes he and his mother as having been intolerably close: "We have been like one, so sensitive to each other that we never needed words. It has been rather terrible and has made me, in some respects, abnormal" (Moore, 1962, p. 69). A man's efforts to individuate from his mother and the difficulties he experiences when the mother holds him tight, interfering with his ability to become his own person, have already been addressed in the theories of Stoller and Glasser. There is ample reasons to assume Rupert's philosophy and fear of involvement are comparable to that of the author. Gerald's parents are complete opposites of Lawrence's own parents: Gerald's father is warm, his mother cold and distant.

It seems likely that Lawrence himself had, for a time, feared the consequences of loving a woman, imagining it might replicate the dangerous liaison he had with his mother. This we glean from the way Lawrence portrays Rupert as a man terrified of declaring his love for Ursula, fearing that doing so might spell the beginning of the end in that it would likely lead to the loss of his vitalizing sense of independence and autonomy. Rupert is wary of love; he dances around the question of whether he loves Ursula, much to her chagrin. Rupert insists that Ursula work to maintain her own sense of autonomy and independence were they to wed. After all, Rupert's previous woman friend, Hermione, had desperately needed him to provide form, substance, and meaning to her vacant state of being, and Rupert has no wish to repeat such a ghastly experience this time around.

Rupert spells out the dangers of losing oneself in the process of "becoming one" with one's mate:

> Fusion, fusion, this horrible fusion of two beings, which every woman and most men insisted on, was it not nauseous and horrible … Why could they [he and Ursula] not remain individuals, limited by their own limits? Why this dreadful all-comprehensiveness, this hateful tyranny? Why not leave the other being free, why try to absorb, or melt, or merge? One might abandon oneself utterly to the MOMENTS, but not to any other.
>
> (Lawrence 1920, p. 200)

Such thinking calls to mind Emmanuel Ghent's paper in which he distinguishes *surrender* from *submission* (1990, p. 111):

> [Surrender] is an experience of being "in the moment," totally in the present … Its ultimate direction is the discovery of one's identity, one's sense of self, one's sense of wholeness, even one's sense of unity with other living beings. This is quite unlike submission in which the reverse

happens: one feels one's self as a puppet in the power of another; one's sense of identity atrophies. In surrender there is an absence of domination and control; the reverse is true in the case of submission (Ghent, 1990 p. 111)..

While Rupert strives to maintain a modicum of independence within the context of marital union, Gerald hungers for a type of union that both threatens and promises to obliterate one of the two as autonomous beings. Gerald desires *to be* loved but seems incapable of loving. His domineering ways, his incorporative desires threaten to subsume Gudrun:

> He seemed to be gathering her into himself ... drinking in the suffusion of her physical being, avidly. He lifted her, and seemed to pour her into himself, like wine into a cup. "This is worth everything," he said, in a strange, penetrating voice.
>
> (Lawrence 1920, p. 215)

In other passages, Gerald tires of his existence and seeks to disappear into Gudrun. By the time the tale ends, we realize only one of the two will survive the relationship.

The relationship between Rupert and Gerald is complicated. They are as close as two men can be—so much so that readers are left wondering whether their bromance is homoerotic in nature. While they might indeed be bisexual, each man appears chiefly heterosexually inclined. Rupert tells Gerald: "We are mentally, spiritually intimate, therefore we should be *more or less* physically intimate too" (Lawrence 1920, p. 272, italics added to emphasize ambiguity). Gerald announces: "I don't believe I have ever felt as much *love* for a woman as I do for you" (p. 275). The two proceed to wrestle naked before a fire—a scene highly suggesting they had gone a long way, if not all the way, toward engaging with one another at least bodily, if not sexually.

There can be little doubt that Lawrence's writing was influenced by the writing of Sigmund Freud, which was widely discussed amongst European intellectuals at the time.[1] Lawrence was introduced to Freudian thinking by his wife, Frieda von Richthofen (Lawrence)—a free-thinking feminist who, in 1907, had had an extramarital affair (one of many) with Otto Gross, one of Freud's more notorious colleagues. Gross, who was analyzed by Carl Jung, championed women's rights and the freedom to do as one pleased sexually. Gross introduced Frieda to Freud's enlightened attitudes about sexuality and sexual freedom, which she—in turn—passed along to Lawrence. She wrote:

> I had just met a remarkable disciple of Freud [Gross] and was full of undigested theories. This friend did a lot for me. I was living like a

somnambulist in a conventional set life, and he awakened the consciousness of my own proper self.

(F. Lawrence, 1935/1983, p. 1)

Writing about her first encounter with Lawrence in 1912, Frieda noted: "We talked about Oedipus and understanding leaped through our words" (F. Lawrence,1935/1983, p. 2). Their eventual marriage was Oedipal in nature. When the two first met, Lawrence's bride-to-be—several years his senior—was married to one of Lawrence's former professors. A month after they met, Lawrence and Frieda fell madly in love and eloped, leaving behind Frieda's former husband and the couple's three children.

Lawrence was predisposed to be intrigued with the Oedipal concept given the nature of his relationship with his own mother, about whom he wrote: "we have been great lovers ... [we] loved each other almost with a husband and wife love" (Moore, 1962, pp. 68–69). In his essay "Parent Love," Lawrence outlined how such an "Oedipal victor" type relationship is "poison for the boy" (1922, p. 174),[2] in that it suppresses the boy's independence, it leaves him grappling with "exaggerated sensitiveness alternating with a sort of helpless fury" (p. 166) that seriously interferes with his ability to develop loving relations with women once the boy becomes a man. Lawrence wrote, as if addressing his own mother, about the unfortunate condition such a boy encounters when he enters puberty:

> Instead of waking now to a whole new field of consciousness, a whole vast and wonderful new dynamic impulse towards new connections, it finds itself fatally bound. Puberty accomplishes itself. The hour of sex strikes. But there is your child, bound, helpless. You have already aroused in it the dynamic response to your own insatiable love-will ... You have got your child as sure as if you had woven its flesh again with your own. You have done what it is vicious for any parent to do: you have established between your child and yourself the bond of adult love ... All your tenderness, your cherishing will not excuse you. And this is fatal. It is a sort of incest. It is a dynamic spiritual incest, more dangerous than sensual incest, because it is more intangible and less instinctively repugnant. Of course, parents can reply that their love, however intense, is pure, and has absolutely no sensual element. Maybe—and maybe not. But admit that it is so ... the intense pure love-relation between parent and child inevitably arouses the lower centers [sic] in the child, the centers of sex.
>
> (Lawrence, 1922, pp. 168–169)

While this passage reflects Lawrence's thinking about his own experience, he did not consider it his alone; rather, "the tragedy of thousands of young men in England" (Moore, 1962, p. 161), so Lawrence presents what might be regarded as his thesis about the psychopathology of a certain type of mother–son relationship.

A careful reading of two of Lawrence's novels leads one to the conclusion that such thinking served as the basis for both *Sons and Lovers* and *Women in Love*. The title of *Sons and Lovers* is telling: The mother of the novel's main character, Paul Morel, forges an incestuous-like relationship with her son, ostensibly making him her lover. Once grown, Paul's fiancée battles Paul's mother in an effort to wrest Paul from her grip, only to lose out when the mother develops cancer and Paul breaks off his engagement to tend to his dying mother—a detail that precisely parallels Lawrence's own life.[3] Lawrence experienced his mother's possessiveness as oppressive: "Nobody can have the soul of me. My mother had it, and nobody can have it again" (Moore, 1962, p. 70).

Jean Laplanche proposed a "general theory of seduction" based on what he called the "fundamental anthropological situation," which touches on themes Lawrence spelled out in his essay "Parent Love." Laplanche describes what he deems to be a universal condition wherein the mother's sexual unconscious, drawing upon infantile residues, "compromises" the messages she sends to her son in her dealings with him. Such residues—infantile sexual drives—inevitably become stirred up in the mother as she ministers to her child. As a result, her adult-seeming messages become enigmatic communications that the boy must translate in whatever way he does, doing so at several points along the way as he successively works to make sense of the meaning of her communications. Laplanche (2011b) writes in a way that echoes what Lawrence had written:

> To my mind there exists a fundamental difference between the *sexual drive* of childhood and what surfaces at the moment of adolescence, which is effectively the emergence of the *sexual instinct*. The sexual instinct then catches up with the drive, which has developed over many years, and there is between the two a serious problem of coherence and cohesion and, most importantly, of content. (p. 105, italics added)

What is radical in Laplanche's thinking is its decided environmental focus—how maternal seduction, short of outright sexual incest, sets in motion "a confusion of tongues" (Ferenczi, 1933) that inevitably and universally results from the mother's infantile sexual unconscious that shapes the boy's experiencing of his sexuality and his gender identity.

Knowing about the nature of Lawrence's relationship with his mother informs our reading of *Sons and Lovers* and *Women in Love*. Lawrence felt both drawn toward and repelled by his mother; he felt a powerful need to break free of her crippling grip. Writing in her memoir about her life with D. H. Lawrence, Frieda Lawrence confirms what readers of the former's works are likely to have gleaned about his feelings about women. Frieda reports his having told her, "If my mother had lived, I could never have loved you, she wouldn't have let me go," and then adds: "In his heart of hearts I think he always dreaded women, felt that they were in the end more powerful than men. Woman is so absolute and undeniable" (Lawrence, 1935/1983, p. 50).

In his novella *The Captain's Doll*, Lawrence spells out the dangers a man faces with a woman who has designs on him and plans to use him to serve her own needs, perhaps reflecting how Lawrence himself felt used by his own mother:

> And you can say what you like, but *any* woman, today, no matter *how* much she loves her man—she could start any minute and *make* a doll of him. And the doll would be her hero: and her hero would be no more than her doll ... If a woman loves you, she'll make a doll out of you. *She'll never be satisfied till she's made your doll.* And when she's got your doll, that's all she wants. And that's what love means.
>
> (Lawrence, 1923, p. 175, italics added)

Here, we hear echoes of Masud Khan's idea of how a mother turns her boy into her idolized idea of who and what he must be to her and for her, an idea that is also in concert with Lacan's thinking.

In *Women in Love*, the literal question "what does Woman want" is posed twice, years before Freud posed that question in his correspondence with Marie Bonaparte (Gay, 1988). In *Women in Love*, Lawrence writes in the third person about how Rupert thinks about mothers and—by extension—about women in general:

> She wanted to have, to own, to control, to be dominant. Everything must be referred back to her, the Great Mother of everything, out of whom proceeded everything and to whom everything must finally be rendered up. It filled [Rupert] with almost insane fury, this calm assumption of the Magna Mater, that all was hers, because she had borne it. Man was hers, because she had borne him ... *Man must be added on to a woman before he had any real place of wholeness.*
>
> (Lawrence, 1920, p. 200, italics added)

At this juncture, it proves instructive to consider the particulars of Lawrence's upbringing. His mother was a highly educated, literature-loving woman who, by Lawrence's account, despised her husband: "Their marriage life has been one carnal, bloody fight" (Moore, 1962, p. 69). His mother belittled the boy's father, a barely literate coal miner who frightened his young son. While Lawrence despised his father on Oedipal grounds, we surmise he faulted him as well for failing to save the young Lawrence by plucking him from his wife's clutches. Having never established a close, loving bond with his father, Lawrence might have left home suffering from "father hunger" (Herzog, 2001), manifesting in a desire to establish close, loving bonds with men.

With this background in mind, let us delve more deeply into the storyline of *Women in Love*. As the novel begins, Rupert is in a long-term relationship that fuels his skepticism about the viability of loving relations in general. His lover, Hermione, suffers mightily from an inner sense of lack as outlined by Lacan.

> She [Hermione] had no natural sufficiency, there was a terrible void, a lack, a deficiency of being within her ... She craved for Rupert Birkin. When he was there, she felt complete, she was sufficient, whole. For the rest of time she was established on the sand, built over a chasm ... If only Birkin would form a close and abiding connection with her, she would be safe during this fretful voyage of life.
>
> (Lawrence, 1920, p. 9)

Hermione needed Rupert more than she loved him, which turns out to be true of Gerald's draw to Gudrun as well. Gerald and Hermione appear to be male and female versions of the same type of person insofar as both are incomplete beings who need another to complete them. Perhaps these are male and female versions of Lawrence's possessive mother, who one gets a sense needed him and used him to help establish herself as a full living being.

Hermione's internal vacancy precluded her from having anything sub-stantive to give Rupert. He found her dependency revolting, and in the end they hated each other's guts. We suspect such parasite-like behavior might have been comparable to what Lawrence sensed of his mother's need for him. Thus starts the arc of Rupert's story. Hermione's clinging possessiveness is something Rupert must escape, but whether he can succeed in forging a more viable, loving relationship with another woman remains to be seen. This then, I would submit, defines Lawrence's personal and literary task to navigate. Lawrence notes: "One sheds one's sickness in books" (Moore, 1962, p. 234).

As the story progresses, the peril of becoming involved with a woman is illustrated when Gerald's sister, Diana, drowns in a small lake situated on the family's land. When the lake is drained, Diana's body is found. Her arms are tight around the neck of the local doctor's son, pulling him under to his death. The message could not be clearer. The character of Rupert, with whom Lawrence appears closely aligned, is searching for a way to *surrender* to love without *submitting* wholly to a woman or succumbing to the suffo-cating constraints of conventionality. Rupert struggles against his loving impulses, hoping to stave off the peril of personal annihilation. He fears that If he were to tell Ursula he loved her, each would end up melding into the other, becoming like-minded individuals who aren't in fact individuals in the strict sense of the term. Rupert cannot risk doing anything of the sort, so he dedicates himself to maintaining a sense of himself as a self-defined and self-determined individual with a separate subjectivity and an unrelenting ability to think for himself.

Rupert is equally concerned about becoming limited by committing to a single person:

> If you are walking Westward, you forfeit the northern, eastern, and southern direction—If you admit a unison, you forfeit all the possibilities of chaos ... if you enter into a pure unison, it is irrevocable, and it is never pure until it is irrevocable ... *Love is a process of subservience.*
>
> (Lawrence, 1920, pp. 152–153, italics added)

Here, we encounter a line of thinking familiar to many clinicians who treat marriage-aged men who struggle with the task of committing themselves to a woman, fearing what they will lose in the way of future options by doing so.

To avoid the perils of merger, Rupert seeks to forge an altogether different type of arrangement with Ursula—one he hopes might prove psychologically survivable. He tells Ursula he is looking for something *beyond* love, a joining together that spares each partner's individuality. At first, Ursula is baffled by what Rupert is proposing. She worries he is trying to subjugate her to his way of thinking—that he is bullying her much in the same way her father bullied her, that being the transference aspect of their relationship. At other times, Ursula is patient with Rupert's philosophizing, though perturbed and hurt by his reluctance to declare his love. Eventually, Rupert realizes it is possible to accept "*the obligation of the permanent connection with others*" and to permit himself to surrender "to the yoke and leash of love" without forfeiting his individuality. Ursula, in response, comes to realize what Rupert seeks benefits both—that he is seeking a union that lies beyond domination and submission. This distinguishes Rupert from Gerald in that Gerald views all relationships through a lens of domination and submission, and he has every intent to bend Gudrun to his will.

As it turns out, the breadth of Rupert's needs could not fully be satisfied by being married to a woman. He wanted to be "blood brothers:" with Gerald: "That is what we ought to do" [Rupert] tells Gerald. "We ought to swear to love each other, you and I, implicitly and perfectly, finally, without any possibility of going back on it." Gerald demurred: "We'll leave it till I understand it better" (Lawrence, 1920, pp. 206–207). It is debatable whether Rupert's desire for male closeness represents latent homosexuality or is something more sublime and transcendent. After all, Lawrence most likely suffered from father hunger (Herzog 2001, 2004) and was hungering for male involvement having had a father about whom he wrote: "I was born hating my father: as early as I can remember, I shivered with horror when he touched me" (Moore, 1962, p. 69). Furthermore, if Rupert/Lawrence loved both a man and a woman, he might be spared the accompanying peril of putting all his eggs in one basket were he to become dependent upon Ursula alone. In Act 3 of *Hamlet*, Shakespeare writes: "Where love is great, the littlest doubts are fear; When little fears grow great, great love grows there." Lawrence himself could not imagine surviving the loss of his dear Frieda, writing: "If she left me, I do not think I would be alive six months hence" (Lawrence, 1935/1983, p. 134).

The arc of Rupert's psychological development swings upward as the story proceeds, while that of Gerald gradually plummets. Gerald's relationship with Gudrun turns sadomasochistic, much as Rupert's relationship with Hermione had been when the story first began. As the novel progresses, it becomes increasingly clear Gerald is incapable of loving a woman, though he seeks *to be* loved by one. Gudrun notes:

> Every woman he comes across, he wants to *make her in love with him*. He doesn't even know that he is doing it. But there he is, before every woman he unfurls his male attractiveness, displays his great desirability, he tries to make every woman think how wonderful it would be to have him for a lover. His very ignoring of the women is part of the game ... He should have been a cockerel, so he could strut before fifty females, all his subjects ... his maleness bores me. Nothing is so boring as a phallus, so inherently stupid and stupidly conceited.
>
> (Lawrence, 1920, p. 463, italics added)

Gerald's unceasing need to dominate—to exert control over others—stands in the way of his ability to form a mutually loving and respectful relationship with Gudrun. He sees all relationships as singularly configured in zero-sum game fashion: One wins or dominates; the other loses or submits in "doer/ done to" fashion (Benjamin, 1990; Davies & Frawley, 1994). Gerald dominates in all his dealings with others. In an early chapter, he exerts sadistic control over his horse, which clearly is terrified by the noise of a passing train. Gerald forces the mare to endure his terror to show the horse who is boss: "And if your will isn't master, then the horse will master you," to which he adds, two pages later, "and woman is the same as horses" (Lawrence, 1920, pp. 139, 141). Gerald seems to manifest clear-cut signs of toxic masculinity, particularly in comparison to Rupert, who is a very different kind of man.

As domineering and masterfully powerful as Lawrence paints Gerald as being, in the end, he turns into a helpless baby rooting for the breast, seeking sustenance denied him by his cold and distant mother. Over the course of the story, Gerald becomes lost—spiritually bankrupt, staring into the void he sees reflected in the mirror, terrified by the emptiness of his soul. He has no idea about how to remedy the "misery of nothingness," the "stress of this hollowness" (Lawrence, 1920, p. 266), which makes him sound very much like Hermione. After his father dies, Gerald sleepwalks his way into Gudrun's life. She receives him—more out of pity than love—and realizes he needs her to save him from himself, from having to face who he is at his core. Towards the end of the novel, Gerald recognizes that Gudrun is self-sufficient, whereas he is an incomplete and unfinished being. Gudrun wonders to herself: "What then! Was she to be his mother? Had she asked for a child, whom she must nurse through the nights, for her lover ... An infant in the night, this Don Juan?" (p. 466).

Gerald imagines introjecting Gudrun's goodness, drinking her in to fill his empty vessel; he also imagines evacuating his badness into her: "Into her he poured all his pent-up darkness and corrosive death, and he was whole again. It was wonderful, marvellous, it was a miracle ... he was lost in an ecstasy of relief and wonder" (Lawrence, 1920, p. 244). Gerald seeks to become spent, to be drained of his inner tension. Here, Lawrence sounds very much as if he is writing about the death instinct—another of the many themes developed in *Women in Love*.

Before concluding this chapter, we must consider the question of the legitimacy of examining a writer's work in the context of his personal life story and, on that basis, forming conclusions in the belief they may apply to men in general. This was, after all, how Sigmund Freud worked—mostly using patient material, though sometimes studying pieces of artwork or a famous individual's life story as the basis upon which to draw conclusions about human psychology. Oftentimes, his cases (e.g., the Ratman, the Wolfman) were more clinically extreme in nature, which nonetheless did not keep Freud from generalizing based on a single case study as he worked to fashion a general psychology.

In the case of D. H. Lawrence, I believe D. H. Lawrence's Oedipal-victor type relationship with his mother, while not the norm, nonetheless presents psychological consequences that arguably are generalizable. One of my first control cases was just such a man—a married father of three who, as a child, spent his nights keeping his mother company while her husband was traipsing about from county to county as a travelling salesman who didn't return home until his selling week was over. As the eldest boy, he and his mother would "put the kids" bed, after which she'd speak intimately with her son, who she treated as the man of the house, about her many secrets, much to his delight and chagrin. Like Rupert (and Lawrence as well, since he openly discusses how fond he was of men), my patient experienced a powerful homosexual transference to me, which became the central theme of our work together.

What is remarkable about Lawrence's depiction of these two types of men is how close he comes to arriving at conclusions about male psychology that decades latter would be made by psychoanalysts. Both Stoller and Glasser envisioned boys and men struggling to establish and maintain a sense of their autonomy against the gravitational pull exerted by the combined effect of the mother's desire to keep her boy near and the boy's own wish to remain within his mother's sphere. The life and work of D. H. Lawrence conforms to the theories these men proposed to explain the unique developmental challenges boys face as they individuate from their mothers. It also comports with theories advanced by Khan. Finding data that lies outside the realm of psychoanalysis proper proves helpful to the extent it can be thought to constitute confirmatory evidence coming from sources not dedicated to supporting theories proposed by the leaders. While D. H. Lawrence was acquainted with Freudian thinking, he can hardly be considered a devotee. In fact, he was a vocal critic of psychoanalysis, which becomes apparent when reading certain of his essays. When it comes to the damaging nature of the type of childhood Lawrence was made to suffer, he threw down the gauntlet, challenging analysts to explain how psychoanalytic treatment can undo such extraordinary damage of the sort he had been made to endure at the hands of his father and mother.

Notes

1 Lawrence was friendly with David Eder and Barbara Low, two early psycho-analytic practitioners in England; and he was well acquainted with members of the Bloomsbury Group, a forward-thinking collective of artists and intellectuals who actively discussed many current matters, including Freud's "new psychology," which advocated for more liberal attitudes about sexuality.
2 Lawrence had not used that precise term, though what he describes amounts to what that term designates. Being an Oedipal victor is bittersweet: One feels, at the same time, triumphant, narcissistically gratified, guilty, and an imposter to the extent one knows one can never fully fill the father's shoes (Gil, 1987; Halberstadt-Freud, 1991; Lasky, 1984).
3 "Muriel is the girl I have broken with. She moves me to madness and demands the soul of me. I have been cruelling to her, and wronged her, but I did not know" (Moore, 1962, p. 70).

6 Variations on a Theme
The "Doing To" and "Being Done To" Forms of Perversity

The nature of men's sexual fantasies ranges from those in which the man is doing something to another to ones in which something is being done to him by another. "Doing *with* another" is an entirely different matter, one that is closely associated with one's capacity for mutual recognition/genuine inter-subjectivity. The degree to which "doer/done to" dynamics (Benjamin, 1990) define a man's approach to relating is directly proportional to the degree of his perversity, remembering Robert Stoller's proposition that every man's fantasy is at least a bit perverse.

When a man fantasizes about or acts the part of "the one who is *doing the doing*," what often gets expressed are cruel and sadistic impulses to control, demean, diminish, humiliate, entice then deny or refuse (tease) the other in the "zero-sum game" belief there are only two roles one can play—to wit, that one is either the victim or the victimizer, a belief closely associated with toxic masculinity. When a man's preference is to picture himself or position himself masochistically vis-à-vis another—on the receiving end of treatment that leaves him feeling controlled, demeaned, diminished, humiliated, enticed, then denied (teased) by another—he submits to and endures the mistreatment as an understood (agreed upon) condition of engagement (Wurmser, 1993, 2007). The arrangement leaves the man feeling disempowered, at the mercy of the other who mercilessly abuses him. The fact the man is more actively engaged in authoring such treatment is something he both knows and tries hard to not know.

"Doing to" and "being done to" varieties of pornography roughly correspond to Stoller's two theories about the root causes of perversity. If a boy has trouble individuating from his mother, experiences a threatening desire to be reunited with her (Glasser), or feels threatened by his need for a woman or her power over him, that man will likely become sexually aroused by the prospect of doing this or that to whomever (sadism), which supports his sense of masculinity by emphasizes instrumentality over receptivity. On the other hand, if a boy had been narcissistically traumatized early in life, by being shamed for his outward masculine displays, he is likely to become sexually excited imagining a reply of that experience, an instances of the "done to" type sexual fantasy (masochism).

DOI: 10.4324/9781003609339-6

"Doing to" and "being done to" roughly correspond with Freud's concept of sadism and masochism (1905, 1910, 1915a), which are two sides of the same coin. Which of the two roles one prefers to play in one's fantasy life—whether it plays out in one's mind, in the porn one watches, or through one's interactions with others—depends on the function of the fantasy and, hence, the psychology of the man. Stoller insisted that a man's sexual fantasies hold the key to understanding his entire character structure, which explains why he was so keen on exploring the topic in such detail.

The raw data Stoller relied upon to develop his theories about sexual fantasy (which he preferred to call "erotic plots") did not draw as much from his work with patients as it did from those he referred to as his "informants." Stoller's study of pornography, which contributed to his understanding of the function of sexual fantasy, developed quite accidently in the early 1960s when a "transvestite"[1] man (heterosexually oriented, cross-dressing man) dropped by his office in the Neuropsychiatric Institute at the University of California at Los Angeles School of Medicine and dropped off some "materials" for Stoller's edification: pornographic magazines the man collected and found highly sexually arousing. At the time, Stoller had no interest whatsoever in what the man had to offer, and two years lapsed before he retrieved those materials from his desk drawer and decided to seriously study what the pornographic storylines that were pictured might say about this man's sexual desire—a man who went on to become one of Stoller's chief "informants."

Stoller obtained and studied other examples of transvestite-oriented pornography, which led to his realizing that the stories each of these samples told were remarkably similar: all were of the "being done to" brand of pornography—though Stoller did not use that descriptor, instead sticking with the more familiar term "masochism." Stoller (1975) described a prototypic storyline in this fashion: "a frightened, pathetic, defenseless boy-man finds himself, through no fault of his own, trapped by powerful, dangerous beautiful women, who bully and humiliate him … forcing him to put on women's clothes" (p. 66). This marked Stoller's introduction to the study of pornography, which he quickly realized could serve as "a biopsy" of a person's psychic life. It was then that pornography "became for me an efficient and surprising entre into understanding erotics" (Stoller 1993, p. 4).

While Stoller knew much about masochism, he soon learned about the sorts of narcissistically traumatizing experiences boys suffer early in life that contributed to their proclivity to repeat those experiences in fantasy and through watching a specific brand of pornography. When such boys grow to be men, they chiefly identify with the boy-man pictured in the pornography who is being humiliated by the women. These men also identify with the aggressors—those who torture him. After all, he authors the fantasy (even by dint of selecting such porn for viewing), which places him in league with his torturers. This double identification makes the viewing of a re-enactment of a past trauma something that is now taking place in the patient's mind, whether self-generated or portrayed through the medium of pornography.

The imagined repetition of the trauma is less traumatizing by virtue of the man's agency (he imagines it in his mind's eye or picks it to watch), his identification with the aggressor, and the fact the action replays at a safe enough distance from the original traumatizing event, helping ensure it does not seem too real—for if it were to feel real, it would likely re-traumatize him. *The man wants to get close but not too close to the original event.* One's orientation to a past trauma is often of this nature. Because the boy-man is pictured as being forced, he/the viewer cannot be accused of wanting this to happen—that is the illusion. "The trick is to take the power to humiliate away from someone who can spring it on us unexpectedly and therefore traumatically," noted Stoller (1975): "We do this by becoming, ourself, the one who controls the mechanisms, no longer helpless ... *one humiliates oneself to avoid being humiliated*" (p. 30, italics added). Is the man a masochist, a sadist, or a bit of both? After all, he simultaneously identifies with the victim as well as the victimizers, pictured as powerful women whose accoutrements are symbolically suggestive of penises. These are, accordingly, women with penises ("phallic women"), women who miraculously possess elements of both genders.

Stoller undertook an extensive investigation into the childhood experiences of the man who had first introduced him to this type of pornography. He conducted in-depth interviews not only with the man but also with several family members who had been present and could help corroborate what the man remembered having experienced when he was young. What became apparent as a result of this investigation was the fact this man (and others like him, as it turns out) experienced the following history: Early in life—around the age of four, once the boy had established a sense of himself as male and masculine—powerful female caregivers intermittently had dressed him in girls' clothes then laughed at the sight of his having been turned into a girl, *deeply bruising the boy's male pride.* These female caregivers experienced the boy's burgeoning boyishness as an "irritant," which triggered their envy, leading them to humiliate the boy by intermittently crushing his male pride in this cruel fashion.

In that this humiliating event was highly traumatic, one would expect this to be the last thing the man would want to revisit, let alone incorporate into his favored sexual fantasy; but this is precisely what happens. In imagining the traumatic event by fantasizing about it or by watching pornography that replicates key elements of it, the man orchestrates it. His authorship cannot be denied, yet must be denied to create an illusion that it is happening to him all over again; but this time the man is *mastering it through the act of repeating it,* which is the essential reason he gravitates to using this psychic device. Stoller suggested such an enacted erotic plot provided the viewer with a sense of having triumphed over the woman who had victimized him in this fashion. The scenario rewinds the tape and replays the past traumatic event. In that the viewer *repeatedly survives the re-experiencing of the event,* he triumphs over his original abusers. He has not been defeated; he shows himself as potent—he gets aroused and erect—proving his maleness survived and remains intact, damaged but not destroyed. In this way, pleasure replaces anguish. That is the essence of Stoller's theory.

Cuckold Pornography

This leads us to consideration of a second type of "done to" pornographic storyline—one Stoller would have had a field day studying were he to have known about it at the time. This type—referred to as "cuckold pornography"—is similar to the sort of transvestite pornography Stoller studied, differing only insofar as transvestite porn involves two roles (the tortured boy-man playing one role, the group of women constituting a second collective role), whereas cuckold pornography involves three distinct roles: 1) the tortured man ("the cuck") with whom the viewer closely identifies; 2) a second man (the "bull"), pictured as being amply endowed; and 3) the cuck's girlfriend or wife, who, as the story unfolds, has sex with the bull in plain sight of the cuck, having made clear the bull is more to her liking. The cuck is humiliated, having been deemed inadequate and unworthy relative to the bull, who witnesses the cuck being humiliated, turning it to pure shame. To make matters worse, the woman rubs it in. She belittles and humiliates the cuck by declaring that the bull has what the cuck lacks: sexual prowess, superior equipment, and the wherewithal to satisfy her in ways and to degrees the cuck never could—a cruel and devastating critique that torpedoes the man's self-worth as a man.

An internet search will find plenty of examples of men drawn to this type of "done to" pornography. For example, one man writes:

> My addiction is of cuckold pornography, particularly humiliation. But I don't want this, it's sick. I get off on it, it's incredibly sexual, but it would kill me if it happened in real life with my current girlfriend. Sometimes I think of her dressing up for a bull (a stronger lover) and getting penetrated by him with me watching … I try to shake these thoughts out my head. The porn itself is really unhealthy as it affects my self-esteem and is very psychological.

Permit me to outline conclusions gleaned from my clinical experience that led me to recognize certain factors that can contribute to a man's becoming drawn to watch this type of pornography. These men experience an intense compulsion to watch such porn repeatedly; it is like an itch that can never be relieved no matter how hard the man scratches. If we work backwards, taking as a starting point the pornographic storyline of the man being belittled and humiliated because he cannot hold a candle to another man, who the woman deems sexually superior in comparison, we can engage in a bit of reverse engineering to piece together what might be at work here. I am not referring here to any given patient; rather, I am demonstrating how one might develop a hypothesis about the dynamics operating behind the scenes that leads such men to watch cuckold pornography.

Imagine, for a moment, a mother who sends conflicting messages to her son: at one moment, she explicitly belittles and demeans him; at another moment, she acts as if she favors him over the father, making him an "Oedipal victor," which both pleases and disturbs the boy. One can easily imagine how confusing this would be for the boy, who doesn't quite know what to make of the mixed messages. The boy's sense that he is preferred by his mother over the father leaves him feeling both proud and guilty at the same time. He believes himself responsible for having proven himself superior to his father—a man he loves, respects, and admires—which leaves him feeling guilty and in need of being punished, even if he has to author it, which becomes his want. Restitution required the boy-turned-man to suffer the role of "cuck"—the role to which he imagines his father had been relegated when his mother invited her son in, and he lacked the wherewithal to resist the invitation. If it were solely the case that a mother treats her son as an Oedipal victor, the way D. H. Lawrence's mother seemed to have, without intermittently treating him in ways that attacks the boy's sense of self-worth, we would not expect such a man to be attracted to such porn.

Replaying the traumatic conditions, this time around with the man in the driver's seat (he chooses it, hence he authors it), retells the tale to make it seem as if "the truth of the matter"—that he had suffered injurious, traumatic mistreatment at the hands of his mother over which he had been powerless—*was a lie*, which demonstrates how perverse individuals rearrange facts to suit their need with the aid of illusion. In this retelling of the tale, it was *he* who had made his mother say those awful things to him, *he* who seduced her—*that* was the truth of the matter; hence, *he only had himself to blame*. Such reasoning echoes Fairbairn's (1952) "moral defense," which entails the child's assuming badness to preserve the goodness of authority figures: "better to be a sinner in a world ruled by God than a saint in a world ruled by the Devil" (pp. 66–67).

The way adults use fantasy or fantasy-based pornography to help rectify the effects of childhood trauma is like the way children use "play" to help them work through the challenging and traumatic aspects of life. But, just as play sometimes becomes pathological when it endlessly replays the trauma rather than helping work through it, the same is seen in the use of sexual fantasies and pornography that attempts but fails to rectify the trauma once and for all.

An example of the non-productive use of play was provided by Lenore Terr (1979), who studied the psychological effects on the 26 children (aged 5–14) who were involved in the 1976 Chowchilla, California, kidnapping—hijacked from their school bus and forced into a lightless trailer buried deep underground. The ransom attempt was foiled when the bus driver and two of the older boys succeeded in prying open the roof of the trailer, enabling everyone to escape. Initial reports suggested the children had suffered no ill effects from the trauma; but Terr discovered that every one of the children was haunted by what they had lived through, collectively suffering from post-traumatic stress disorder (PTSD). Their habit of re-enacting the hijacking event in "play" only led to further re-traumatization in a vicious cycle sort of way. I would suggest men attracted to cuckold pornography comparably achieve no lasting psychological gain, which leads them having to watch the pornographic scene play out over and over again.

The Play's the Thing

Each of the two examples of "done to" porn just considered involve more than mere naked bodies doing their thing—more than still or moving images. Stoller was keen on the importance of the story itself, the unfolding tale that excites some but not others. He believed the pornographic storyline—the "erotic plot"—was key to understanding what the viewer has come for, what he is wanting from the watching, what he is needing to work out.

Stoller was fond of playing a little trick on each incoming class of psychiatric residents. He would put them through the paces to drive home his point that specifics of a given man's fantasies makes all the difference when it comes to sexual arousal and desire. Before a room full of mostly male psychiatric residents (and I can attest to this from first-hand experience), Stoller would project an image on a screen of an attractive, full-breasted, naked lady with her hands strategically cupped over her genitals. With the audience's attention trained on the image, Stoller then presented a kaleidoscope of descriptors to demonstrate the way different attributes demonstrably alter how excited one becomes *with the idea* of who the woman is. Stoller (1985b) would invite the audience to play a bit with the image:

> We look at her; the photo stays the same, but you are going to change. For I tell you she is a starlet, a harlot, the farmer's daughter, your neighbor's daughter, your neighbor, unmarried, married, divorced, American, French, eighteen, twenty-eight, a farm girl, a city girl, five feet two with eyes of blue, six foot two with a size 12 shoe … She is a student in your seminar on epistemologic hermeneutics, a cheerleader, an airline stewardess posing for Playboy, a mud wrestler. She is lesbian, straight, bisexual, oversexed, nymphomaniacal but frigid. (p. 45)

You get the idea. Depending on the nature of one's fantasy life, sexual arousal rises and falls as a function of the woman's particulars. But just when you think Stoller has made his point, he goes in for the kill: "In fact, none of these is true. The reason her hand is hiding her genitals is not to simulate modesty but because she is an unoperated transsexual male" (Stoller, 1985b, p. 45). Touché!

Let's next consider a fantasy that excites a surprising number of women; though, at first glance, we wouldn't expect it to given that the scenario pictures an event that is the last thing any women would want to be forced into experiencing. Research conducted worldwide, replicated several times over, establishes that a third of the women surveyed had sexual fantasies picturing themselves being raped.[2] By no means does this suggest women want to be raped or like being raped. Rather, these fantasies tell a story that attests to the woman's overwhelming and irresistible attractiveness. She drives men wild with lust: They cannot help themselves; they have no choice but to force themselves on the woman sexually.

While "rape" fantasies typically picture the woman being forced against her will, *her active authorship of the fantasy*, along with the pleasurable excitement she experiences imagining such a scene, tells a different story. Actual rape is the furthest thing from her mind. In the fantasy, it is her desirability that is driving the man wild; accordingly, she is the one in control, though illusion pictures it otherwise. While actual rape expresses a man's power over women, rape fantasies covertly express a woman's power over men. She dominates, though the fantasy makes it appear otherwise.

It is alarming to think some men fantasize about raping a woman, particularly if one doubts the man's ability to limit such urges to fantasy alone. Stoller (2009) observed that "most men who fantasize rape would be impotent in the real situation, because reality has so many loose ends, while daydreams, including pornography, are tailor-made to exclude the unpleasant complications, fears, and impotencies the world brings" (p. 210). There is a world of difference between a man who fantasizes about domination and a man whose dealings with women reek of domination, which we would consider a perversion. A man might invite his sexual partner to help him act out his domination fantasy by proposing she play along (e.g., schoolmaster/innocent student) but this is another matter altogether, seeing that the unfolding events are mutually satisfying and consensual. If the woman is so inclined, the game begins with one condition: If things begin to feel too real, the woman can blow the whistle and the enactment will end at a moment's notice. Such a contract allows lovers to proceed safely as they venture into a potentially grey zone between fantasy and reality.

The "Doing to" Form of Perversity

Next, let's consider an example of "doing to" pornography, paying close attention to the storyline given what has just been said. A patient of mine, an unmarried artist in his late 30s, recently described to me his preferred brand of porn. The genre is called "mall cop porn," and the specific type my patient was drawn to watch goes something like this: A "buxom blonde" (note how that term fetishizes her) has been caught shoplifting and is in a compromised (one down) position relative to the mall's chief security cop who has caught her red-handed. He has compassion for the predicament she finds herself in, which was of her own making. She had been a bad girl and must pay the price. In my patient's preferred version, the cop is willing to show mercy and suggests a quid pro quo exchange. He does not have to turn her in, and explains he is open to making a deal, which arouses the viewer's excitement. The cop has power over his prey and can "get" her to do what he wants to satisfy his sexual desire. Spicing up the scene is the woman's portrayal of someone who recognizes she is powerless—and, maybe, is even excited by it. The fantasy reverses the man's anxiety of being comparably caught powerless in a disabling web created by a woman's attractiveness and the power she exerts over him.

My patient was sexually aroused by this storyline for reasons highly personal in nature. Here, I will be speaking in generalities rather than divulge the specifics of his inner life. The porn he watches is sadomasochistic in nature—specifically, a man is in a dominate position vis-à-vis a woman who's been caught in a compromised position with little say over the matter ("I've got you right where I want you"). It is important to note this man's sexual relations with the women in his life bore no resemblance to what he enjoyed imagining and watching performed on screen, establishing the disconnect between fantasy and a man's actual sexual behavior when with living, present beings.

Centerfolds and Pinups

Stoller seems to overstate his case when he declares that every man's sexual fantasies are—to whatever extent—perverse, and all male-oriented pornography expresses hostility directed towards the featured women who are pictured being treated in controlling, demeaning, cruel, and humiliating ways (e.g., forced to do as she is told, rendered powerless, in no position to say "no," made to feel soiled, and so on and so forth). But what about the type of "soft porn" that adorns the pages of *Playboy* or *Hustler*? Surely such images don't convey hostility toward the women who seem so innocently pictured.

"Centerfolds" and "pinups"—that is what the women featured in these photos are often called, as if reduced to mere fetishized imagines—are objectified and dehumanized, as if the woman's outer shell is all the man needs to see; all he wants to know of the woman, since knowing anything more about who she is (aside from the scanty bio written to titillate) stands a fair chance of tainting the illusion of who the man needs to believe the woman to be. That was Stoller's argument, which he graphically illustrated by throwing out varying descriptors as the room full of residents laid their eyes trained on what turned out to be a biologically male individual awaiting a sex-change operation. Erasing the woman's particulars—those things that make her who she is—is in the service of letting her be whomever the man needs her to be to pique his arousal. Perversion entails objectifying women by focusing on certain of their parts (e.g., their body parts) rather than relating to the entirety of their being. A woman's physical appearance is a fraction of what a man might "take in" when he is with a living and breathing female being.

Lots of questions spring to mind. What *storyline* might implicitly accompany a nude photo? In what way is the pictured woman a victim? Stoller (1975) insisted: "There is always a victim, no matter how disguised: no victim, no pornography" (p. 65). Finally, we might wonder what *early trauma*—humiliation, frustration, deprivation—gets psychologically addressed and mastered by looking at "nudies." Whatever it might be, it must be universal given that every man is a voyeur at heart.

As you might imagine, Stoller had answers for every one of these questions. The deprivation? Stoller noted Westerners live in societies of covered bodies, leaving boys with an unfulfilled desire to look at nude female bodies to their heart's delight. What young boy wasn't titillated by *National Geographic* photos of bare-breasted women walking about with baskets balanced on their heads? Western culture doesn't permit boys or men to stare too long at a woman's body without being slapped (literally or metaphorically) or labelled lascivious. How exciting is it, then, to have an opportunity to gawk at a woman's naked body *for as long as one wants*—to one's hard delight? Porn, after all, is voyeuristic in nature—it involves *what* one is seeing, what one *is getting* to see, what one is *getting away with* seeing.

Who is the victim? Stoller suggests a storyline: The man viewing the porn is imposing his wish to look at a woman who is powerless to say "no." Granted, she sat for the photo; but that detail is beside the point. Illusion makes it seem otherwise. The story is one of robbing the woman of her privacy, of her ability to keep from men what men so desperately desire to see. So, there is the victim and there is the story. But what is the underlying childhood trauma/frustration that is being addressed by *possessing* porn— "possessing" being the operative word. A pornographic image creates an illusion that the woman is possessed by virtue of the fact the man has a naked photo of her and there is nothing she can do about it! The varied manifestations of sadism include the man's attempt to possess another human for his own use or exert undue control over others.

Beyond being deprived of the wish to see women's bodies, which fuels the desire to feast one's eyes, is another trauma Stoller fails to mention in relation to pornography, though he addressed it in the context of talking about men's efforts to maintain their sense of autonomy as they grapple with the captivating lure of women—their ability to entice—which extends far beyond women's sexual allure. Stoller proposed a man must succeed at the task of breaking away from his mother so that he can then become a man— not "mommy's little boy." Managing and mastering the feared and desired task of becoming autonomous risks a man's identity as a man should he succumb to the strength of his desire for union. Possessing a woman (by having her photo) rather than *being possessed by a woman* is also part of what gets addressed by having a woman's naked photos in hand—one's prized and private "stash." Here, the difference is "having" (a picture) rather than "being had." The "pinup" is like a butterfly caught and then pinned to a board, motionless, owned. Themes of domination and control can be found as an underlying story in this form of porn as with many other forms.

An additional subliminal thrill, which accompanies viewing others having intercourse, is symbolic: getting to watch Mommy and Daddy go at it—the primal scene that most of us would dread seeing, and were excluded from seeing, to our relief and dismay. Stoller (1973) includes this in his list of the victims portrayed in porn: "The victims then are the 'grownups,' whose lack of omnipotence [which the child had once presumed to exist] is proved since they do not know they are being observed" (p. 88).

Notes

1 Here, I am using an outdated term to accurately reflect Stoller's thinking using the precise terms he used. Stoller (1975) differentiated this form of cross-dressing from that which is done: 1) for the sake of entertainment ("drag queens"); 2) to reflect a male-appearing individual's core sense of identity as girl/woman (transsexuals); or 3) as an act of subversion (men who don women's clothes and walk about looking the part, all the while knowing and appreciating the fact there is a male organ dangling beneath the dress). By comparison, the man who engages in the perverse act of erotic transvestism, noted Stoller, acts male, considers himself a man, engages in heterosexual relations, and lives life comfortably as a male. He is, however, sexually turned on by dreaming up or watching pornographic portrayals of a highly specific erotic scenario that replicates the original, fantasy-originating humiliating experience.
2 Twenty separate studies conducted since the mid-1990s involving over 3500 subjects report women having routine fantasies of sex scenes in which they are forced to submit to a powerful man (e.g., Critelli & Bivona, 2008; Kanin, 1982; Pelletier & Herold, 1988; Strassberg & Lockerd, 1998).

7 Internet Porn (IP)

A Place to Hole Up and Hide Out

Since the advent of the internet, every man can easily access an extraordinary array of pornographic content. No matter how unique a man considers his proclivities to be, he can always find internet porn (IP) that closely corresponds with his favored fantasies. Nowadays, accessing porn is just a "click" away. One no longer needs to drive to the local porn shop, Nowadays, one can watch as much porn as one likes right in the privacy of one's home. Cooper (1998) attributes the popularity of IP to three chief features: *access, affordability*, and *anonymity*. To this list, Young (1999) adds *convenience* and *escape*, and Delmonico (2002) adds two important features: *intoxicating* and *isolating*.

A 2024 review by Pornhub, the webs premier internet porn (IP) hosting and streaming site, reported that IP viewers on average go online and finish up at breakneck speed—the average viewer gets on and gets off these sites in 9 minutes and 40 seconds flat.[1] While most men indulge in IP with no ill effects, 3–6 percent of male viewers develop serious dysfunctions due to heavy and compulsive consumption (Kafka, 2010; Odlaug et al., 2013; Ross et al., 2012). Many such men find themselves down a rabbit hole, confined to their rooms, spending inordinate amounts of time each day sitting before a screen, wasting precious time that could be better spent. An over-reliance on IP correlates with a tendency to withdraw into a world of fantasy (Boies et al., 2004; Sweet, 2014; Toronto, 2009; Young, 2007). For some, IP substitutes for sexual relations with others (Paul, 2005). Referral patterns to London's Portman Clinic found that, in 1998, only one patient was referred for treatment of the compulsive use of IP; five years later, this condition was amongst the most common problems cited in referrals to the clinic (Morgan & Ruszczynski, 2018).

Men who are at greatest risk of developing "porn addiction"[2] are emotionally and psychologically predisposed by virtue of their feeling depressed, anxious, emotionally stressed, and/or interpersonally challenged, leading them to turn to porn to help self-regulate ("self-soothe") their internal states.[3] Heavy use of IP sets in motion a "vicious circle when the feelings of self-hatred and inadequacy [that heighten the amount of time men watch IP] are further reinforced by the very attempts at lifting them via the pornography" (Woods, 2013, p. 308). Wood (2011, 2013, 2014) describes how perversion

DOI: 10.4324/9781003609339-7

in general, and IP in particular, constitutes an efficacious escape from the twin perils associated with relating to others, resulting in an individual's withdraw from object relations not just to protect oneself from the dangerous whims and aggressions of the object, but also to protect one's objects from the destructive effects of one's own aggressiveness.

Male versus Female Porn

The content and function of male-oriented and female-oriented porn share little in common. Men by and large are not drawn to porn that features romantic themes or portrayals of one's being overpowered by sexually excited men; women, on the other hand, are not typically drawn to porn that pictures subjects being treated in a cruel and sadistic fashion—a common feature of male-oriented porn. Unlike male fantasies and male-oriented pornography, female fantasies tend to portray emotional intimacy and affection. "A woman's aphrodisiac is a man's soporific," Stoller (2009, p. 186) aptly noted.

The function of pornography differs depending on the gender of the viewer. For men, porn helps rectify ("triumph over") past traumas, particularly those that involved a threat to the boy's sense of masculinity (Stoller, 1975), following the formula: "I am humiliated; I discover revenge; I humiliate; I have mastered the past" (Stoller, 1991, pp. 47–49). Men also use porn to redirect their sadistic impulses (to harm and/or control), which can be discharged by watching hostility-themed pornography. In this manner, porn can help prevent such impulses from manifesting (or manifesting only to an attenuated extent) when interacting with one's sexual partner. Women occasionally use porn to help them manage past traumas; but they are not inclined to use porn to mitigate the effects of pent-up aggression that threatens the strength of their bond with their lover.

Stoller (1975) made a provocative claim relative to male-oriented pornography: "There is, I allege, no nonperverse pornography, that is, sexually exciting matter in which hostility is not employed as a goal" (p. 86). Stoller was clear about the matter. Male fantasies are perverse by nature, given the extent to which they fetishistically objectify women and picture them being treated in a hostile manner, portrayed as harmed, demeaned, humiliated, and belittled, forced to submit to such mistreatment.

Stoller proposed that men's fantasies, which are directly tied to the types of porn a man likes to watch, develop chiefly in reaction either to childhood trauma or to the feared effects of one's urge to merge with the archaic mother figure, which stirs up the man's aggressive impulses. Traumas include: the "ego"-crushing[4] experience of being humiliated, belittled, demeaned, controlled and rendered powerless (e.g., a boy dressed in girls' clothes); intolerable frustration caused by being overstimulated by an early childhood object (e.g., frequent exposure to a naked mother); and intolerable deprivation that robs the child of the ability to satisfy certain forbidden sexual desires (e.g., to masturbate to his heart's delight or to look at naked bodies for as long as he wants). One might assume such traumatic conditions occur infrequently, which would make perverse male fantasies infrequent; but Stoller thought otherwise, believing such conditions are more routine than commonly thought.

Oftentimes, what a man likes to see performed on screen and what he is comfortable doing with his sexual partner have little in common. While porn watching reflects an inability to get from one's sexual partner what one can get from watching porn, it would be a mistake to imagine it ought to be otherwise—that a woman should be a man's lover and his fantasized porn star at the same time. Efforts to meld the two generally fail since men, by and large, don't want the women in their lives to have to endure the sorts of demeaning or degrading acts they love watching play out on screen. Men turn to porn to get something they cannot get, and that generally cannot be gotten (even "should not be gotten"), from their sexual relations with real beings. This point I cannot overemphasize, given that it represents the essence of what I am trying to convey in this chapter.

Additional Psychoanalytic Perspectives on Porn

Psychoanalytic writers have tended to view the motives behind a man's overindulgence in internet porn as being defensive in nature[5]—driven by a fear of the dangers associated with interpersonal relationships. Toronto (2009) described porn as a place in one's mind that is "sequestered, outside of time, intensely private, which provides men a way of psychically *retreating* from life—from the slings and arrows of outrageous fortune (painful memories, awareness of one's deficits, feeling helpless, the risk of interpersonal rejection, and so on and so forth). One escapes to a place wherein men "attempt to exercise control and aggressively capture the supplies they lack" (p. 131), akin to what is portrayed in Sendak's (1963) picture book *Where the Wild Things Are*, a retreat to a land where one has total charge.

While John Steiner (1993) never addressed the phenomenon of IP, his concept of "psychic retreat"—a place where "they retreat behind a powerful system of defences which serve as a protective armour or hiding place" (p. 1)—aptly describes the sorts of defenses that are at work when a man relies heavily on IP, which becomes for him a hideout that protects him from exposure to overwhelming levels of psychic pain.

Pauley (2018) described pornography as providing a "cordoned-off realm" (p. 135) within the mind—a retreat into a state of (seeming) self-sufficiency, which constitutes something akin to a manic defense against the depressive position (the realization that one ultimately needs others). He sees pornography functioning as a kind of

> toggle switch ... that allows the individual to shift between different self and body states as a temporary means of self-regulation/self-soothing,

which works to an unprecedented degree, providing a source of sooth-
ing during solitary moments of intense anxiety and fragmentation. (p.
137).

Understanding the sadomasochistic (S&M) aspects of IP requires one consider more than just the nature of what is taking place on screen—the story's
content (e.g., a man treating a woman in a highly sadistic fashion). Pornography involves actors/objects who can immediately be summoned, like the
genie in a bottle. They appear and reappear at the viewer's whim—they
have no "say" in the matter; they need not be ready or "in the mood." They
are under the viewer's complete control, called forth at the exclusive dis-
cretion of the viewer, who expects to hear the magic words: "Your wish is
my command." This level of absolute control and availability is a feature of
IP that also contributes to its expression of S&M tendencies.

Turning-the-Tables Porn: *The Devil in Miss Jones*

Stoller (1975) illustrated his theory about pornography with the aid of a
classic porn storyline: "A woman who starts out cool, superior, sophisticated,
and disinterested but is swept [by the man] into a state of lust with monu-
mental loss of control" (p. 88). This passage was written coincident with, and
may well have been written in response to, the release of one of the best-
known and highly acclaimed porn films of all time—*The Devil in Miss Jones*
(1973). The storyline of that film neatly aligns with Stoller's assertion that the
perversity of pornography manifests in the portrayal of a woman being
harmed, punished, tortured, humiliated, dominated, and so on and so forth.
By the time the film ends, Miss Jones is in a tortured state—conditions prevent her once repressed but now inflamed level of sexual desire from gaining
satisfaction. But we are getting ahead of ourselves, having skipped to the end
without relating the tale.

Miss Jones is a lonely and unhappy woman in her 30s who has lived a
virtuously chaste but empty life. She cuts her wrists, assumes she will be
welcomed into heaven, but learns otherwise—her suicide disqualifies her,
relegating her to remain in limbo forever. She begs to be allowed to return to
earth to earn her way into hell, and her wish is granted. Thus starts her sin-
based, devil-inspired pursuit of sexual pleasure that is portrayed in a series of
increasingly lust-driven, making-up-for-lost-time scenes, capped off by a
thrilling threesome. That does the trick; but hell, for our Miss Jones, involves
her eternal existence confined in a small room with an impotent man whose
sole interest is catching flies.

What sort of trauma might make this pornographic storyline particularly
satisfying for certain men? When the curtain rises, the audience is introduced
to a woman who is sexually unavailable to men who might fancy her—
making her the uninterested party about whom Stoller wrote. The man's
desire is thwarted; try as he might, he lacks control over the situation.

Nothing he does makes a difference—he is impotent, given that the woman is utterly unresponsive to his efforts to woo her.

Two things happen as the story unfolds: The woman loses control over her sexual desire and, in the end, over the circumstances of her existence; she is made to suffer a degree of sexual frustration *comparable to what the man had suffered at the hands of an unresponsive woman*: "Look who is suffering *now* from a lack of control and unsatisfied desire!" This we might call turning-the-tables type porn. Any number of different childhood traumas could sensitize a man to the experience of feeling powerless, teased, and psychologically challenged by the task of coping with intolerable levels of unfulfilled desire.

"Porn Addiction": *Don Jon*, a Cinematographic Example

It can take quite some time for a man to find, as he surfs the net, something that approximates his fantasy, which helps explain why some men lose track of time caught up in a search for porn that will hit the spot. Wood (2013) contrasts a man's disappointment when he fails to find, in the outside world, conditions that closely replicate his fantasies with what is achievable when the man turns to cyberspace: "the internet allows the individual to scan vast numbers of images, with the likelihood … [he] will eventually find quite a close match" (p. 166).

Real-life sexual partners have subjectivities of their own. They have preferences, desires, and wishes they expect to help determine how the sex act plays out—which can interfere with a man's hope his fantasy will play out without having to be modified or watered down by the expectations, hopes, preferences, or desires of his sexual partner. As a result, porn "delivers" in a way a real woman cannot (and had better not, for her own sake). Hence, for some men, real-life sexual relations cannot hold a candle to the unmitigated excitement of seeing one's favored fantasies played out on screens of one sort or another, with cell phones predominating.

Pornography provides a skewed and objectified view of what women should look like and how they should behave, potentially paving the way for disappointment that can infect real-life sexual encounters. In an ideal world, the woman is always ready and willing, submits freely whenever propositioned, and is easily aroused—eliminating any chance the man's "ego" will be bruised or his sexual tension left unspent. In an ideal world, the man gets hard and stays hard, and pumps away for as long as it takes to bring the woman to orgasm. But things don't always play out as expected, and pornography muddies the waters by causing some men to expect actual sexual encounters to replicate what they'd seen on the screen. There are two additional ways that heavy porn watching might negatively impact a man's sexual relations with women: 1) excessive indulgence in porn might deplete the strength of the man's sexual drive, which some men need to overcome the anxiety of pursuit; and 2) supercharged on-screen sexual portrayals of sexual prowess and carnal bountifulness might excite men to no end—quite literally—making encounters with actual sexual partners pale by comparison.

What porn delivers is analogous to what Tinbergen (1989) termed "supernormal stimuli"—artificially created stimuli that *mimic but intensify* the visual features of naturally existing stimuli (see also Barrett, 2010; Hilton, 2013; Toates, 2014). Such supernormal stimuli can override the natural, expected, evolution-promoting behaviors of animals. For example, artificial bird eggs that are made to look larger and more colorful than actual eggs attract mother birds, who select the more vibrant, artificial eggs to sit on, ignoring the very eggs they themselves laid. Tinbergen created artificial butterflies with larger and more colorful wings, and male butterflies repeatedly tried to mate with the artificial butterflies in lieu of actual female butterflies.

Internet pornography can be thought to operate in comparable fashion to the extent film makers work to create illusions about the degree of sexual arousal each actor achieves and the availability of sex partners who are rarin' to go at a moment's notice and are never distracted by their own issues nor disinclined to engage sexually because they are too peeved or hurt to be sexually responsive. IP is quite effective at creating an illusion that makes it appear *as if* one's prayers have been answered that one's most exciting and satisfying fantasy have been actualized. To the extent "as if" falls away, porn is rendered real—a sleight-of-hand trick. Things play out *without a hitch*, akin to Erica Jong's (1973) "zipless fuck."

All of what's just been said comes to life in *Don Jon* (2013), a movie that portrays a man with a porn addiction. Written and directed by Joseph Gordon-Levitt, who also plays the lead role of Jon Martello, the storyline is about a proud Italian-American man in his early 20s who speaks with an exaggerated New Jersey accent. Porn had taught this boy-man a thing or two (but not nearly enough) about what a sex partner should look like and be like, and how she should behave, given what he'd seen enacted on the screen.

Jon Martello is a lady-killer, which earns him the nickname "Don Jon," a takeoff of you-know-who. Jon is a sexual machine; he runs through a string of one-night stands portrayed comically by his use of carbon-copy type maneuvers that lead viewers to believe he is merely going through the motions, a man with a method—behaving in such a tediously repetitive fashion that one never sees a glimmer of his humanity. Go to work, pump iron, masturbate to porn, go to confession, lay a chick, repeat.

Like the proverbial revolving door, the movie provides a kaleidoscope of impersonal sexual encounters, none of which, Jon makes sure to let us know, matches the level of arousal and release provided by pornography, which is so much better—cleaner—than actual sexual encounters because there is, in Jon's words, "no smell, no taste." Jon's actual sexual encounters are punctuated by his repeated retreat to the computer screen—he even sneaks off to watch porn as the girl he'd just "laid" moments before is asleep in his bed. It appears that Jon cannot get his fill of IP, even when he has just had sexual relations with a real human being.

Jon meets his match when he becomes smitten with a girl named Barbara (played by Scarlett Johansson), who, in short order, busts him by checking his internet search history—something Jon didn't even know existed. Barbara tells Jon she is thoroughly disgusted by his dirty little habit. Jon fires back, "All men watch porn, and any man who claims otherwise is lying." He futilely mansplains—sexual relations and masturbating to porn have nothing to do with one another—but Barbara is having none of it. She is deeply offended and demands to know "Why am I not enough to satisfy you?" Barbara has no intention of being put in a position (for that is how she sees the matter) of having to compete with the likes of what Jon sees on screen; so she lays down the law, leaving Jon no option but to comply, though he suffers a withdrawal reaction abstaining from watching IP. His belief that being a man means not taking orders from anybody, particularly women, is suddenly called into question. From this point forward, Jon stays on the straight and narrow, as we learn more about the effect porn has had on his beliefs about how sexual relations should play out.

Jon objectified every woman he slept with in accordance with what he'd seen portrayed pornographically. His objectifying tendencies included *self-objectification*: Early in the film, Jon sees himself along culturally determined, highly stereotyped lines that dictate what it means to be a man—a point expressed in the film by the inclusion of animated clips used effectively to drive home the point that Jon is functioning as a comic book character. In her own way, Barbara is equally fetishistic: She engages in a form of objectification that spells out how real men should act based on cinematographic portrayals of men she'd seen on screen. Rather than think for herself, she adopts a culturally determined model about manhood, mistaking fantasy for reality. Barbara cannot accept genuine aspects of Jon that do not align with her fantasy of what makes a man a man, which places the two on a collision course, each lost in their own limited versions of reality and manhood.

The arc of the story has Jon seeing the light with the aid of Esther, a somewhat older woman he befriends (played by Julianne Moore). Esther reveals herself as a full, living and breathing being who experiences a range of feelings, which forces Jon to see her for who she is—a woman beyond his limited ideas about women. This encounter awakens and redeems Jon, who transcends the narrowness of his ignorance that had entrapped him in the guise of a comic book character he had previously mistaken himself as being.

The Secret Lives of Men

Don Jon had a secret—one he wished to keep hidden, one he never expected would be discovered or would require him to justify his hidden habit. The way women react upon learning the man in their life has been watching porn ranges from a "boys-will-be-boys" type shrug to unmitigated outrage based on the belief the man has committed an indisputable and unforgivable act of infidelity. There is no "right" reaction for a woman to have given the circumstances. What the man's habit says about him, about the nature of his relationship to women, and the quality of his relationship with the women in his life is very much open to debate as to what the event comes to mean to his girlfriend or life mate.

In most instances, the sorts of sexual imaginings a man uses to "get himself off"—with or without the aid of porn—differ considerably in comparison with the types of sexual acts he feels comfortable engaging in with his lover. Most often, a man thinks twice about introducing the level of sadism pictured in male pornography into his sexual dealings with his partner. If the man dares propose the couple try out what he'd seen acted out on screen, his proposal, overall, meets with mixed reactions and may even blow up in his face.

A highly romanticized fairy-tale like concept of a long-term partner is that of the "smitten" man who finds his lover so attractive that he wants for nothing, and accordingly ceases to have eyes for others. While it is unlikely one could find a woman willing to admit she thinks as much, one senses that some women—Barbara in *Don Jon* being one such woman—do appear to think along these lines, whether they admit it or not. Such thinking primes women to be duly outraged at the mere hint that their man could—as former US President Carter admitted in a *Playboy* interview—"look on a lot of women with lust," admitting he'd "committed adultery in my heart many times."[6] Such statements are best contextualized by noting that Carter's 77-year marriage to his wife Rosalynn was rock solid.

The fragile nature of long-term romantic bonds is seriously challenged by literal acts of infidelity. No woman wants to feel she is being forced to compete with the likes of another woman who leaves her wondering whether she is all her husband or boyfriend wants and needs. Perhaps *that* other woman (or, by extension, the women pictured in porn) is more to his liking—a painful narcissistic blow, an intolerable slap in the face the woman feels must be put right.

Kernberg's (1991, 2011) concept of an "excluded third" fits in nicely here—the proposition that a couple must eliminate any hint of a potential rival to help solidify their long-term bond. Each party knows there exists, somewhere out there, a partner who is better suited, more attractive, and better able to satisfy their partner's sexual needs in comparison to themselves, but it is best this "third" go unmentioned:

> Every man and every woman unconsciously or consciously fears the presence of somebody who would be more satisfactory to their sexual

partner, and this dreaded third party is the origin of emotional insecurity in sexual intimacy, and of jealousy as an alarm signal protecting the couple's integrity.

(Kernberg, 2011, p. 235)

An idealized version of a close, intimate bond with another often involves the concept "we have no secrets"—that is, we hold nothing back from one another, we "come clean," we tell our partner everything. Some readers may align with such thinking. But giving oneself away to such a degree—at least in the minds of some men—can seem tantamount to a loss of the man's sense of existing as a separate being aptly portrayed in D. H. Lawrence's *Women in Love*. When a couple strives to achieve the ideal of complete openness and honesty, the results can prove disheartening, illustrated in the lines of Carly Simon's 1972 poignant, Grammy-nominated song "We Have No Secrets"—which appears to refer to her failed marriage to James Taylor:

> We have no secrets,
> We tell each other everything
> About the lovers in the past
> And why they didn't last
> We share a cast of characters from A to Z
> We know each other's fantasies
> And though we know each other better when we explore
> Sometimes I wish
> Often I wish
> That I never knew some of those secrets of yours …
> In the name of honesty, in the name of what is fair
> You always answer my questions
> But they don't always answer my prayers.

The Divided Minds of Men

Many men feel compelled to find ways to keep themselves from unleashing their innate propensity for hostility and aggression, which is considerably stronger in men than it is in women. Beyond testosterone, male aggression is piqued by several different factors: to counter the gravitational pull of mother/mother figures and/or the man's own desire to regress, to merge with women; to express outrage at the mother for having betrayed her son by sleeping with Daddy; a vengeful response to having been injured, teased, belittled, rendered powerless, and so on and so forth when they were young. Such aggression is experienced as a threat to the boy/man's relationship with his much-needed object, leaving him grappling to find a solution to the dilemma. One solution involves the creation of a divide within the minds of men that helps keep their aggressive impulses from entering into their dealings with women toward whom they chiefly feel tender, loving affection. This divide is largely facilitated by men keeping select aspects of their beings hidden, and pornography is one place where such needs are permitted to exist and be expressed.

Glasser (1979, 1985) proposed that an important factor contributing to the generation of perversity—with male pornography being one amongst many forms of perversity—is man's existential struggle to maintain his sense of autonomy in the face of a regressive urge to merge with the primal mother. According to Glasser's "core complex theory," this struggle is considerably harder for boys and men than it is for girls and women, given that males feel distanced from their mothers by virtue of their gender differences—a factor that heightens the desire to get back with mother.

Aggression helps a man survive the regressive pull exerted by a mother's unrelenting hunger for union with her child and/or her son's urge to merge. When this aggression becomes sexualized, it takes on a sadomasochistic hue. As Ruszczynski (2018) noted,

> The sexualizing of self-preservative aggression results in sadism, a wish to hurt and to control. In fantasy this preserves the object, which is now no longer threatened with destruction but is engaged with, albeit sadistically … [which] acts like a binding force, organizing and securing the object relationship. (pp. 29–30)

Men who feel their autonomy and their masculinity is threatened by the degree to which they are open with and close to women conclude that defending their autonomy and sense of masculinity requires they institute a modicum of secrecy to protect a cordoned-off part of their being from being exposed or invaded. No matter how close a man is to his partner, she is denied entry to this private compartment of the man's mind. For some men, porn represents just such a compartment. That isn't its chief function; rather, it is a secondary function, in accordance with Waelder's (2007) concept of multiple functions.

The degree to which men feel a need to compartmentalize—to keep a side of themselves secret—varies. While some men are more forthcoming, more comfortable opening up to others, others remain remarkably reticent, fearing the vulnerability that comes from letting others in. The greater the need to retreat, the greater the impulse to watch porn, with porn watching constituting a threat to a man's ability to form relations with others.

Freud (1912) described the extent to which men are internally divided between two impulses or instincts: on the one hand, the *base urge* to ravage a woman's body in a violent and hostile fashion; on the other, a path many men consider the "high road"—treating their partners in a most loving, tender, and affectionate fashion, which men often conclude precludes them from demeaning the women they love by getting "down and dirty" with them. This was, after all, what Freud (1912) was driving at in his paper "On the Universal Tendency to Debasement in the Sphere of Love": "Where they love [affectionately, tenderly] they do not desire [carnally, do not treat sadistically] and where they desire, they cannot love" (p. 1). Put in other terms, the man's base desire to "debase" women (treat them sadistically, "f**k their brains out") is incompatible with the competing desire to love women in a most tender fashion.

Such reasoning led Freud to a "gloomy prognosis [given the] irreconcilable difference between the demands of the two instincts" (1912, p. 190): "however strange it may sound, we must reckon with the possibility that something in the nature of the sexual instinct itself is unfavourable to the realization of complete satisfaction" (pp. 188–189). He considered this condition *a nearly universal aspect* of male psychology, noting:

> There are only a very few educated people in whom the two currents of affection and sensuality have become properly fused; the man almost always feels his respect for the woman acting as a restriction on his sexual activity, and only develops full potency when he is with a debased sexual object; and this in its turn is partly caused by the entrance of perverse components into his sexual aims, which he does not venture to satisfy with a woman he respects.
>
> (Freud, 1912, p. 185)

This theory represents a major contribution Freud made to the psychoanalytic theory of the psychology of the male species.

Freud's description of how averse men are to treating the women they love in such blatantly sadistic fashion ("debasement") is the point Stoller and Glasser would emphasize decades later—the idea that men feel obliged to find ways to redirect such impulses so they don't end up getting expressed toward the women the men love and need, which contributes to an internal divide within the minds of men. Extending Freud's description of this divide leads us to conclude that the sorts of things a man fantasizes about (and the type of porn he likes to watch) and what he feels comfortable introducing into his sexual dealings with his partner by and large remain segregated. This is not to say some men don't move in the direction of introducing sadism into their relationships with their partners; it is only to suggest such matters are relatively uncommon. There is a world of difference between what men like to watch play out on screen and what they want to do between the sheets with their partner. Understanding as much helps clear the confusion that develops in some women's minds when they discover the private lives of their partners.

Kernberg Thought Otherwise

Otto Kernberg (1992) argues that polymorphous perverse infantile sexuality serves an important function in mature sexuality, in that it helps recruit aggression in the service of love. He argues that healthy sexuality includes the ability to tolerate the playful use of "exploitation" of the partner during sexual play: a use of the object that reflects a normal (sublimatory) function whereby the reality of the object relation is maintained while a *fantastic, regressive one is playfully enacted as part of sexual desire and excitement.* Kernberg (1991, p. 48) notes:

> If the couple can incorporate their polymorphous perverse fantasies and wishes into their sexual relationship, discover and uncover the sadoma-sochistic core of sexual excitement in their intimacy, their defiance of conventional cultural mores may become a conscious element of their pleasure. In the process, a full incorporation of their body eroticism may enrich each partner's openness to the esthetic dimension of culture and art, and the experience of nature. The joint stripping away of the sexual taboos of childhood may cement the couple's emotional, cultural, and social life as well.

Kernberg concludes that the inhibition of this sublimatory use of splitting is related to a decrease in sexual excitement and milder forms of sexual inhibition.

Variations on a Theme: Affairs of a Different Sort

Talking about the hidden lives of men leads to a consideration of times when a married man suddenly and uncharacteristically falls for a young, single woman and, in the process, becomes someone he barely recognizes. In the late 1990s, I found myself treating several married men who were having affairs with single women, and a comparable number of single women who had "taken up" with married men. I found this shift in my practice curious, and wondered whether it might have something to do with the news of the day, the Bill Clinton–Monica Lewinsky affair.

The features of these affairs differ considerably from other sorts of affairs. As I listened to the stories these men and women told about how the rela-tionship was progressing (or, more to the point, how it was not progressing), I was struck by how similar their stories were turning out to be—so similar that I began to consider the possibility this pattern of behaviors constituted a bona fide *syndrome*. I subsequently published the results of my research, based on patient interviews and a review of the literature, in a volume enti-tled *The Single Woman–Married Man Syndrome* (Tuch, 2000). After that book was released, patients whose behaviors conformed to what I had described sought treatment, further solidifying my conclusion that such affairs share comparable features and run a predictable course. The stories these men and women told shared certain common elements:

1   The man had not been looking to have an affair. He was taken by surprise, hadn't seen it coming, had not been out looking for any such thing. Cheating was not in his nature.
2   The woman's socioeconomic status is not comparable to that of the man (she has less power, is "one down").
3   The man declares his love and promises to leave his wife, but seasons go by and nothing of the sort ever happens.
4   The man is deeply ambivalent and cannot decide how to resolve the matter. He hems and haws and tries to buy time. He cannot leave his wife, but at the same time cannot imagine remaining married to her. Neither path seems viable.
5   The single woman, who had been patient for the longest time, begins to feel she is being jacked around. From this point forward, the affair runs an emotionally tumultuous course—the woman wants more, she presses, the man resists, and tension develops. In the end, the man *never* leaves his wife and family for this woman. If he and the single woman end up together, this is not an instance of the single woman–married man syndrome. There are instances when the married man does leave his wife, doing so not for the single woman but for another woman, much to the surprise and chagrin of the woman who had patiently been waiting in the wings.
6   The main driving force of the relationship is not sexual; it is more narcissistic in nature. The man's self-valuation receives a heathy transfusion provided by the degree to which the single woman remains devoted to him despite the fact she gets little back in return. She sits by the phone, ready to jump should he find time to see her; but it all feels like crumbs dropped from the table.

What is remarkable about this sort of affair is the extent to which it facilitates the emergence of a formally hidden and sequestered part of the man's personality. The relationship's transformative powers is central to why the man becomes and remains invested in the relationship. It is not so much that he finds the woman amazing; what amazes him is who and what he has become: a man more daring, more adventurous, more fun-loving. This is the story that played out time and again as I listened to the tales these men told about what they were going through at the time.

This syndrome illustrates a phenomenon that primarily is a male proclivity. Men hide parts of themselves away from others, and even from themselves. Occasionally one hears about a man who has two sets of families that live, for example, at either end of a large valley, one knowing nothing of the other. With the single woman–married man syndrome, we see a man being one way with one woman and an entirely different way with another woman. This was cinematically portrayed in *The Captain's Paradise* (1953), starring Alec Guinness as the captain of a passenger ship that travels between Gibraltar, where he lives with his devoted wife Maud, and Morocco, where he intermittently lives with his young, tempestuous lover Nita—23 years his junior. The lives he has with each woman couldn't be more different: Nita and he enjoy an up-all-hours, paint-the-town-red lifestyle, whereas with Maud he lives a respectable, sober existence, with the couple turning in no later than ten.

The minds of men are divided to varying degrees—the phenomenon exists on a continuum. The extent to which men take care to make sure others don't know the likes of them relates to Glasser's "core complex theory," which describes the dangers associated with the prospective loss of a man's sense of self that could result should the man relinquish certain of his self-defining features so he can be reunited with mother.

When Monica Lewinsky's official biographical account of her affair with President Clinton was released in 1999, I was almost done writing my book; and reading her words—which, granted, could be dismissed as mere hearsay—confirmed all that I had concluded about such affairs, having heard the first-hand accounts of both married men and single women. What I found particularly interesting are two things Lewinsky quotes Clinton as having said to her: first, that he was adept at letting others only see select aspects of himself, making sure that no one person ever knew the "true Bill Clinton"; and, second, that he admitted to her, in her words, that he "was increasingly appalled at himself, at his capacity not only for deceiving others, but also for self-deception" (Morton, 1999, pp. 113–114).

Notes

1 https://www.pornhub.com/insights/2024-year-in-review.
2 I am using this term in line with lay thinking about the matter. To date, the profession does not consider "porn addiction" as a recognized diagnosis, given that nothing approximating such a condition appears in either of the two diagnostic manuals—the American Psychiatric Association's *Diagnostic and Statistical Manual of Mental Disorders* (*DSM V*, 2013) or the World Health Organization's *International Statistical Classification of Diseases and Related Health Problems* (*ICD 10*, 2016).
3 See Carnes et al., 2001; Cooper et al., 1999, 2004a, 2004b; Delmonico & Griffin, 2008; Harper & Hodgins, 2016; Pauley, 2018; Privara & Bob, 2023; Sussman, 2007; van der Aa et al., 2009.
4 "Ego" is used here in the colloquial use of the term, synonymous with "narcissism."
5 Or adaptive, seen from an alternate perspective.
6 Robert Scheer, "Playboy Interview: Jimmy Carter," November 1976.

8 Beyond Fantasy and Pornography
An Invitation to Join In

There is a world of difference between a man who arouses himself by the thought of a woman being treated in a cruel, hostile, controlling, demeaning, or humiliating manner and a man who insists women participate in the enactment of whatever it is that turns him on. Some men effectively sequester their hostile and aggressive impulses, taking care to ensure they not bleed into their relations with others; other men appear to have no qualms about forcibly enlisting others to participate in the enactment of such impulses. Robert Stoller believed the vast majority of men are not likely to actualize such impulses; so, whether such fantasies can truly be considered perverse is debatable. I believe It is important to differentiate men who act out their fantasies from those who don't, reserving the term "perversion" for the former, not the later.

If a man asks his sexual partner to participate in the enactment of an S&M that he'd seen on the screen but fails to accurately anticipate how she will respond or becomes ornery when she refuse his request, we are confronted with a man who manifests perverse tendencies. Joyce McDougall (1995) opined:

> In my view, the only aspect of a fantasy that might legitimately be described as perverse would be the attempt to force one's erotic imagination on a non-consenting or non-responsible other ... Perhaps in the last resort, *only relationships can aptly be termed perverse.* (pp. 177–178, further italics added)

Let's consider just such an instance, which emerged during analytic group therapy with patients struggling with the effects of heavy internet porn consumption. The following interaction involves an interchange between a man named "Matt" and other group members:

> "Matt" spoke of his wife's threats to leave him because of his wishes that she should enact the sort of fantasies he has developed through the pornography, rituals of dressing up, domination, and beatings. "But it's only playacting," he said angrily, "so why is she disgusted?" His

DOI: 10.4324/9781003609339-8

problem, he said, was that only by this means could he be sexually aroused, but he also felt he could not live without her. He was confronted by the group about the aggression in his "playacting." They pointed out how he was driving her away and how he himself perhaps had some mixed feelings about his sexual fantasies rather than attributing disgust to his wife. He was also invited to think about why he should even pretend to humiliate his wife. He spoke then about his helpless rage when his mother left him, aged eight, with an abusive father. He connected his fear of his wife leaving him with the loneliness and bitterness at this mother's absence.

(Woods, 2013, pp. 309–310)

"Get a load of this": An Effort to Stun and Disable

Let's consider a type of perversion involving a man's fantasy that escape the confines of his mind and leads him to recruit others to bring his fantasy to life. What I am referring to is the practice of exposing one's genitals to strangers. "Flashers," as they are colloquially called, use aggressive, attention-grabbing means that momentarily disables the victim's ability to maintain sufficient presence of mind to cope with a completely unexpected and incongruous event. The flasher has his victim's undivided attention. Genital exhibitionism amounts to a naked power grab that forcefully places the flasher in a superior "one up" position, relegating the disadvantaged party to the "one down" position. The exhibitionist acts out his fantasy without regard for what the woman wants—or, more precisely, with complete disregard for her rights and wishes. This, I submit, is what turns the flasher on: his ability to leave his victim aghast, stunned, and silenced, unable to think on her feet.

Exhibitionists have the hardest time keeping themselves from repeatedly engaging in such behavior—the recidivism rate is quite high; and, while one might think these men are either psychologically ill equipped to cope with a relatively normal level of libidinal drive or are overwhelmed with an abnormally high sex drive, neither proves to be the case. The flasher's compulsion to expose himself most likely issues from a process of sexualization that makes his actions seem *as if* driven by a powerful drive, which is not the case. Masud Khan (1979) wrote that he had "never met a pervert" whose behavior was driven by "authentic instinctual pressure" (p. 14). The flasher is excited both by the idea of flashing and by the act of flashing itself, excited by all that the act promises to achieve and relieve. The flasher not only exerts control over the victim, but he also maintains his cool while the other "loses her shit"—in a metaphoric sense. This, for the flasher, is a real turn-on. Stoller (1975) noted that what excites the flasher is his ability to be in control while the other loses control.

My interest in exhibitionism was prompted by a patient of mine who revealed, in his second year of treatment, an urge he would indulge from time to time during his teenage years, when he would walk about the neighborhood wearing nothing but a towel around his waist. As an adult, he would lie naked in the backyard of his house, from time to time, in full view of those living in homes overlooking his yard. Assuredly, such exhibitionistic practices differ from those of flashers who are intent on shocking others by displaying their wares, hoping to make a big impression. Rather, I considered my patient an "accidental" exhibitionist. His chance of harvesting a glance was, at best, hit-and-miss; and if, perchance, he caught someone's eye, he would make sure not to let on he knew he had been seen. That would spoil the fun. That was not what he was after. This, I submit, has nothing whatsoever to do with the practices and goals of flashers.

Exhibitionism has different meanings depending on whether the exhibitor is male or female. A woman engaged in exhibitionism does what she can to draw attention to her body. Whether she is looking for anything more than being looked at is left to the man's imagination, and many a man falters trying to figure out whether the woman is eager to make out or is just seeking reassurance that she has the wherewithal to pique a man's interest. Some men have a hard time distinguishing innocent, playful teasing, earnest attempts to tempt, and sadistic forms of taunting. But this feminine variation of exhibitionism has nothing to do with a male flasher who comes looking for something beyond mere looking.

The untoward effect of an exhibitionist's behavior bears no relationship to instances when a woman bears her breasts in "girls gone wild" type fashion. The woman is out having fun, and is counting on those lucky enough to catch a glimpse to be excited by the sight and grateful for the offering. It is playful—teasing—and bears no relationship to instances when a man suddenly exposes himself, which has a completely different effect on the viewer than does a young woman flashing her breasts during a spring break bacchanal.

Such gender differences can be illustrated with the aid of a humorous observation: If a woman undresses in a window and a man walks by and *looks*, he is arrested for voyeurism; if a man undresses in a window and a woman walks by and *sees*, he is arrested for exhibitionism. Intentional looking versus inadvertent seeing—active versus passive—seems to be what makes the difference: the idea that men are inevitable aggressors and women passive victims of an affront. Given that such gender differences exist, my patient would be said to be engaging in a more female variation of exhibitionism.

There is something rather inexplicable and peculiar about exhibitionists. Flasher cartoons—the sort found, for example, in the pages of *The New Yorker*—make light of the act of flashing, as if it were a big joke. One cartoon illustrated the flasher's worst fear: A man in a trench coat, pictured from behind, has his coat fully unfurled, exposing himself to an older woman who gets a full-frontal view. The woman, in response, notes: "Nice lining!" Touché, the perfect comeback. The man had wished to shock; the woman acted as if the only thing she saw that impressed her was an isolated feature of the man's coat—which deflates the man with panache; the exhibitionist is dismayed by indifference (Snaith, 1983).

The absurd nature of flashing makes its alarming nature curious. How can something so comically preposterous be the threat some believe it to be? Isn't flashing a farce? Why is it treated as if it is a big deal? "On the whole," noted Gebhard et al. (1965), "exhibitionists are to be pitied rather than feared" (p. 399). In the past, television newscasters would report "exhibitionist on the loose" stories as if they were on a par with rape; but such levels of alarm were uncalled for given that men who "get off" flagrantly displaying their genitals typically specialize in that act alone; they do not pose the same threat rapists do. Most flashers want nothing more than what they come for (Gittleson et al., 1978; Macdonald, 1973; Silverman, 1941), which leaves us having to explain the terror these men can evoke.

Reading eyewitness accounts of women who had the misfortune of coming face to face with a flasher is eye-opening (Gittleson et al., 1978; Landis, 1956; Macdonald, 1973). These women spell out the "one up/one down" dimension of such interactions. No amount of preparation wholly immunizes a woman when she is caught like a deer in headlights having been exposed to such incongruous, mind-blowing behavior. Siegman (1964) described how the victim is caught off guard by the outlandishness of the man's behavior, which places her at a psychic disadvantage.

Victims of genital exhibitionism describe feeling that they had been rendered mindless and speechless, without a clue as to what to do or say, or how they might get away. Victims of exhibitionism cannot believe what they are seeing—quite literally—as it deviates so much from anything they've ever seen before. Sure, she knew such things happen, but that does not prepare her for this moment. The victim thinks to herself: "This is not happening. This CANNOT be happening. My eyes are playing tricks on me. That's what this must be." Such self-talk is indicative of a momentary state of dissociation not unlike that experienced by rape victims, who psychically remove themselves and watch the unfolding event as if from the third-person position of witness—as if it is happening to someone else.

In fact, exhibitionism is akin to psychic rape. The flasher's victim is robbed of her ability to think on her feet, to adapt to the moment at hand as she routinely had been able to do under less extreme circumstances. It feels to her as if she is being held captive by the sight of what the man is doing. If a man is willing to act in such an extreme manner, God knows what he might do next. The woman reasons she had best keep her eyes on the flasher lest she look away—as if watching somehow controls what comes next.

While each flasher has his own reasons for practicing his craft, in general, all flashers seek to induce comparable reactions from the women they enlist. It is inconceivable that they believe such behavior is capable of enticing or sexually arousing their victims. One would be hard-pressed to come up with a more effective way of stopping a woman dead in her tracks. Though it takes place at a distance and involves no physical contact (Gittleson et al., 1978; Macdonald, 1973), the flasher's actions pack a wallop—the act is quietly violent. The victim gets an eyeful—her sight is assaulted. As analysts, we are drawn to wonder whether the man might be re-enacting a childhood event during which he himself had been forced to see something that was beyond his ability to see and comprehend.

There is little question that exhibitionism is a hostile act intended to evoke powerful emotions in the onlooker, which—in turn—is the source of the exhibitionist's erotic pleasure (Macdonald, 1973). The exhibitionist intends to: "inspire terror" (Christoffel, 1936, p. 323); "fill the mind of his victim with the mixture of terror and sexual excitement" (Sachs, 1942, p. 557); "frighten and shock" (Gebhard et al., 1965, p. 399); "cause fear and humiliation" (Macdonald, 1973, p. 89); "surprise" (Socarides, 1988, p. 471); tease (Sperling, 1947); arouse envy (Stekel, 1952, pp. 163–208); and even embarrass.

The flasher's methods are inhumane, perverse. At a distance, the whole thing seems laughable, but, in the moment, it is no laughing matter. The exhibitionist's actions amount to a wholesale seizure of interpersonal power. The woman is prevented from having much say in the matter. Her attention is forcibly captured and held. Such actions violate the implicit social contract—the unspoken but generally understood rules of interpersonal engagement that dictate that one party must allow the other party's beliefs, wishes, and desires to enter into the equation, to help co-construct how things play out between the two. These rules also dictate that one must respect the other's most basic assumptions about what can be expected from other human beings. No one is to violate another's basic trust by interacting with them in ways that challenge that person's core and orienting beliefs about how humans interact with one another, which could cast serious doubt on that person's understanding of human relations or reality in general.

It stands to reason that the extremity of past childhood traumas experienced by these men most likely is what accounts for the extremity of their actions—their going so far as to involve an innocent other to enact an event meant to somehow reverse the damaging effect of the trauma they had suffered long ago. Stoller (1975) explained how such re-enactments triumphantly turn the tables, a symbolic repetition of the trauma the flasher himself had been forced to endure—how he had been "done to" by a loved one. This time around, with the aid of his victim as proxy, the flasher plays the role of the "doer," relegating his victim to adopt the role he had been forced to play when the original trauma first occurred. Now, he can cause the same shock he had been forced to experience originally. Now, he has proven that he is *not* as invisible or dismissible as he felt when he was young.

A clinical example described by Jacob Arlow, which appears in Chapter 4, bears repeating at this juncture. Arlow described a patient suffering from intense anxiety who combined the defenses of identification with the aggressor and mastering anxiety through proxy. As a child, the patient lived in close quarters with his sister and mother, both of whom exposed him to the disturbing sight of their genitals. He recalled an instance from childhood when he wrapped a piece of black paper around his three front teeth, thus creating the illusion that they were missing (symbolizing a missing penis). The patient then went about his business in nonchalant fashion until his mother noticed and panicked, filling him with glee. He then removed the paper, revealing the hoax, thus reassuring himself in retrospect, regarding his having repeatedly seen his mother's naked body, that "it was foolish of you to be frightened. Once you know the underlying truth you can see that from the very beginning nothing was really amiss" (Arlow, 1971, p. 327). The hoax sadistically created in the mother feelings she had previously aroused in the child, illustrating a point made earlier about the perverse practice of toying with another's sense of reality, as happens when one plays a practical joke on others.

The flasher must know, at some level, that he is engaging in something akin to terrorism—placing another (a woman) at a disadvantage, traumatizing her by forcing her to experience such an unimaginable degree of psychic disability. Most women are not permanently scarred by such encounters, which is not to say they are not deeply rattled at the time, and they may go on to become less trusting of their ability to handle whatever comes their way, come what may. Most often, these men are not conscious of why they are doing what they are doing. Regardless, blatant disregard for the dignity of others is what such behavior telegraphs—which makes the act truly perverse.

Stoller (1985b) pointed out that many exhibitionists are known to hang around after the fact, which has the effect of creating an even bigger stink by engaging the legal system, doubling down on the flasher's efforts to demonstrate, beyond a shadow of doubt, exactly how impactful the sight of his penis had been, thus disproving his worst fears that he is an insignificant being—and man who has nothing to write home about. In his work with exhibitionists, Stoller found evidence that the exhibitionistic act oftentimes is triggered by an instance when the man experienced something contemporaneously wherein someone—a boss, his wife perhaps—interacted with him in ways that caused him to feel ashamed, belittled. Being called to task or otherwise demeaned, which the man might be incapable of psychically processing at the time, results in his sleepwalking his way into enacting yet another instance of flashing. Stoller noted the present-day trauma (being shamed) resonates with an early childhood experience of having been comparably humiliated—a trauma the flasher had never fully processed.

Perverse fantasies are designed to undo and redo past traumas by revisiting the original trauma and introducing elements that twist the story in a direction that provides the fantasizer with a sense of triumph and control in place of the original experience of humiliation, defeat, and powerlessness. When fantasy comes to involve another human, the prospective recruit may not be interested in playing along. Instead, she may veer from the flasher's intended course, potentially leading to a close replication of the original traumatic event, which is the last thing the fantasizer wants to have happen. This then is the exhibitionist's gamble: If the woman he expected and needed to be aghast is instead nonplussed, acting as if what she has seen is no big deal, the exhibitionist has lost the wager and is now worse off for the experience. Just such dangers supercharge the excitement, danger being—in Stoller's theory—an essential ingredient in making the perverse fantasy even more exciting.

9 Perverse Transferences

Perhaps there is no greater challenge to psychoanalytic treatment than that mounted by patients who act as if they understand and accept the core tenets of treatment—what it requires, how it works—but who consistently behave in direct opposition to the analyst's efforts: patients whose "transferences" are perverse in nature. Donald Meltzer (1973), who is typically credited with coining the term "perverse transference,"[1] defines it as an attempt to "displace the analyst from his usual role and transform the [analytic] procedure into a different one, structured by their perverse or addictive tendencies" (p. 136). Such behaviors constitute a destructive attack on the analysis (Riesenberg-Malcolm, 1992), which, in effect, turns the analysis *to shit* ("meaningless")—a term I use to align with Janine Chasseguet-Smirgel's concept of perversion as the disavowal of the father's (e.g., the analyst's) genital capacity and an attack on the order (the way things are, the status quo) by creating an "anal universe" wherein differences of important sorts (male/female, parent/child, sufficient/insufficient)—differences capable of stimulating intense envy—are summarily dispensed with by *homogenizing* and eliminating disturbing variation. In the perverse world, "differences having been abolished, the feelings of helplessness, smallness, inadequacy as well as absence, castration, and death–psychic pain itself—is abolished" (Chasseguet-Smirgel, 1985, p. 13). Such wishful thinking places the perverse patient in direct opposition to the analyst's world view vis-à-vis reality, a battle between –K (what the patient considers knowledge) and K (what the analyst considers knowledge) (Bion, 1962).

In comparison to what analysts typically contend with, treating patients with perverse transferences is another matter altogether. If one is attempting to conduct an analysis, one had best be treating a patient as opposed to an individual who shows up with his sights set on systematically (and infuriatingly) undoing whatever the analyst is trying to accomplish.

To the extent Stoller plumbed the depths of perversion and perversity, he never identified and addressed perverse transferences—patients who go to great lengths to undermine the analyst's efforts. Like most other psychic phenomena, the manifestations of perverse transference exist along a continuum. Occasionally, a patient may relate to the analyst in a perverse

DOI: 10.4324/9781003609339-9

manner but only in circumscribed fashion, without the behavior constituting a full-scale attack on the analysis. At the most extreme end of the spectrum, such perverse patients do not accept treatment as a *mutually agreed upon* means to an end; rather, they consider the events of the analysis an end in themselves—what they came to treatment expecting and wanting to see happen. However, they cannot admit as much at the outset of treatment (perhaps they sense as much themselves, but they are loath to let on that this is what they want because that would be tantamount to showing one's hand to the enemy). Perverse transference implies a lack of a therapeutic alliance; it is all about what the patient is aiming to achieve, which, on the one hand, renders the analyst's agenda a mere distraction in the patient's mind and, on the other, an outline of the lines of attack. To the extent the analyst fails to recognize the truth of the matter—that the patient is attending sessions to get certain of his needs or wishes *directly gratified*, all the while covering up what he is up to—the analysis veers dangerously from the analyst's intended goal.

Joseph (1971) was the first to suggest that the analytic treatment of perversion requires the analyst to discover and interpret perversion as it manifests *in the context of the transference*, which she quickly qualified by noting this all depends on the analyst's ability to "locate" perversion in the transference—an acknowledgment of how challenging this can be for analysts. Etchegoyen (1978) expressed similar beliefs about how the treatment of perversion hinges on the working through of the perverse transference: "In a quasi-satanic way, these patients try to pervert the analytical relationship and test our tolerance; nevertheless, perversion being what it is, we cannot expect anything else" (p. 47). A couple of decades later, Thomas Ogden described the extent to which it had become "accepted knowledge" that the treatment of perversion requires that the analyst identify and help the patient work through the perverse transference.

> [T]he analysis of perversion is not fundamentally a process of decoding and interpreting the unconscious fantasies, anxieties, and defenses that are enacted in the perverse patient's sexual activity. Instead, it has become increasingly recognized that the analysis of perversion centrally involves the understanding and interpretation of transference phenomena that are structured by the patient's perverse internal object world.
>
> (Ogden, 1996, pp. 1121–1122)

Meltzer (1973) noted the extent to which such patients make a concerted effort "to dislodge the analyst from his accustomed role and to convert the entire procedure into one which has the structure of their perverse or addictive trend" (p. 136). By and large, analysts do not expect and are not looking for signs indicating a patient is attempting to triumph over them by deceiving them to accept fabrication as fact (Arlow, 1971). Meltzer noted that the stealth actions of such patients blind the analyst from recognizing that the goal of analysis has been subverted by meeting the patient's objective of gaining direct gratification of his wishes and need to control the analyst—to bully him, to undermine his authority, to pull wool over his eyes, making a fool out of him, and so on and so forth. The patient is gratified by his ability to keep the analyst in the dark.

At some level, the patient knows what he has come for and why he is doing what he is doing. For quite some time, the analyst may go on believing he and the patient are engaged in a genuine psychoanalytic process, when, in fact, nothing could be further from the truth. Joseph (1971) awoke to the fact she had been responding to a perverse patient, who was not particularly forthcoming, by developing "pseudo-insights" that helped organize her own thinking, which she then used to construct "phony" interpretations. By the time the analyst finally catches on to what is happening, which can take years, it is often too late: the subversion has become irreversible (Meltzer, 1973); the patient has done the deed—has attacked the good object and turned it to shit. Otto Kernberg (1992) noted such patients "relentlessly extract what is good in the analyst in order to empty him out and destroy him" (p. 256) deriving conscious pleasure from their destructive engagement with the analyst. They absorb everything the analyst has to offer, and then relentlessly dismantle it.

Perverse transferences have their function: They accomplish several aims that are both defensive in nature (e.g., used to cope with fear of loss of the self or disavowal of reality that causes the patient to feel intolerably envious), and directly discharge the patient's aggressive impulses. Chasseguet-Smirgel (1985) saw perversion in terms of its defensive function: "a balm for our wounded narcissism and a means of dissipating our feelings of smallness and inadequacy" (p. 24). For some people, the raw and direct truth of the matter—which comes from experiencing the totality of another's otherness, their subjectivity—stimulates not only fears of engulfment (being swallowed up by the object to the point of non-existence) but also a host of other primitive fears arising from the object's ability to frustrate and humiliate. Perverse transferences help convince the patient they are in total control, at the mercy of no one. Treating the analyst in a dehumanizing fashion is "the ultimate strategy against the fears of human qualities—it protects against the vulnerability of loving, against the possibility of human unpredictability, and against the sense of powerlessness and passivity in comparison to other humans" (Cooper, 1991, pp. 23–24).

Being able to manipulate the analyst, as perverse patients are apt to do, proves to the patient that he is not at the analyst's mercy with regard to whether the analyst will provide what the patient wants and needs. To the extent the patient senses the analyst will not provide needed psychic supplies or transformative experiences—given his professional dedication to the principle it is best not to gratify the patient's infantile needs, and it is in the best interests of treatment that the patient speak, not act—the perverse patient can make an end run around the analyst's commitment to remain abstinent. Joseph (1971) notes the extent to which this manipulation is not always obvious, in that it can operate in a passive-aggressive fashion. The patient may use words or silence to excite, to sexualize the situation, and/or to destroy the strength of the analytic experience without ever expressing open, active aggression. For perverse individuals, exploitation and manipulation become the chief features of one's relations with others. Bach (1991) writes: "From a certain perspective, one might say that a person has a perversion instead of a relationship" (p. 75).

Less Pervasive Types of Perverse Transference Phenomena

There are perverse ways a patient may relate to the analyst without those moments being indicative of perverse transference. For example, an analysand falls silent and remains so for several consecutive days. Unbeknownst to the analyst, the patient is playing a sadistic game of hide and seek. The analyst, increasingly in the dark about what is going on, stumbles about trying to get his bearings in the absence of data he might use to forge a reasonable understanding/interpretation of what is going on and why it is going on. The analyst grasps at straws to find his way, not knowing the pleasure it is bringing the patient to see him grappling with a state of helplessness like the one the patient had tired of experiencing in his role as analysand.

Sometimes, perverse manipulations develop around paying the monthly bill. I experienced this with two young patients whose parents were footing the bill for treatment. One of the patients—a man in his late 20s—had a way of heightening my expectation that, any day now, he would be bringing payment for the sessions. Each session he would announce his plan (promise?) to bring the check the following session, which developed into a pattern that extended over several sessions in a row. It began to feel as if I was being teased by something dangling just beyond my reach—something the patient knew I wanted. One time when he finally brought the check, he told me not to deposit it until the following week since his mother needed to put the money into his account. That might have been reassuring save for the fact there had been times when the check he eventually brought bounced. This patient was aware of his sadistic wishes to be rough with women and treat them cruelly (having felt frightened of his overbearing mother.

Alfonso Sánchez-Medina presents clinical material along these same lines. While his patient started out paying the monthly bill on time, he began a pattern of presenting the check on the agreed date but requesting the analyst not cash it until a few weeks later. The author writes:

> I managed to understand this by means of the following dream, which [the patient] recounted: "*I was buying petrol for the car, and I paid with a bank note. The shop assistant told me the note was forged, and I*

argued that it wasn't, that it was genuine. Finally, I realised that it was forged but it took a great deal for me to admit this to the shop assistant." The insincerity in payment consisted of the fact that, by paying on the agreed date but requesting that I deposit the cheques later, in reality he was only apparently fulfilling his commitment, and with the argument that he had already paid.

(Sánchez-Medina, 2002, p. 1350, italics added)

More Pervasive Forms of Perverse Transference

Outright examples of flagrant perverse transference can manifest in a variety of ways. The extent to which the analyst catches on, reasonably quickly, to what the analysand is up to can make all the difference in the world.

Treating a phallic narcissist, which arguably is a perverse character type, proves clinically challenging in that it requires the analyst to fashion a treatment approach that differs considerably from how they typically treat neurotic patients. Some perverse transferences are easier to tolerate than others, which largely depends on the intensity of the countertransference reactions that get triggered by the degree and effectiveness of the patient's expressed contempt.

Case 1: Treating a Phallic Narcissist

Michael Diamond (2021, p 40) reported on the challenges he encountered treating a phallic narcissistic man who was incapable of forming and maintaining meaningful relations with men and women—a man who was "full of himself":

A man whose prephallic vulnerability and shameful sense of inadequacy were hidden behind a manic, phallic invincibility—an easily caricatured, militant masculinity in which being "big" through action and power dominated. He overvalued the illusory supremacy of his male endowment while repudiating the feminine, evident in his locating lack in the other and his aversion to "female" characteristics. He repeatedly proclaimed that he did not want to "depend on anyone," and instead, objects (persons and otherwise) were used addictively.

This passage describes well the clinical manifestations of such men who enter treatment seemingly wanting to resolve the root cause of their ailment, but who instead "pervert" their relationship with the analyst. Diamond reported how his patient ostensibly bullied him and expressed unadulterated disdain for him, which had the effect of seeming to turn Diamond into the shameful, inadequate man the patient was trying hard to avoid experiencing himself as being. Diamond's interpretive efforts gave the patient much to scoff at. He called what Diamond provided "psychoanalytic babble"—

which the patient considered a surefire sign Diamond "had nothing real to offer" (2021, p. 42). Eventually, and somewhat predictably, the analysis failed. The author summed up the treatment, noting how it illustrates

> the difficulties of working with an extremely phallic narcissistic man governed by primitive, omnipotent manic defenses operating largely in presymbolic realms. These defenses of phallic supremacy, which served to stave off primordial vulnerabilities as well as castration anxiety, kept him (and his analyst) trapped in a sadomasochistic web that resulted in a limited analysis.
>
> (Diamond, 2021, p. 43)

Case 2: Treating an exhibitionist phallic narcissist

A second case, much like the one Diamond described, involves a man I treated a few decades back, and sheds light both on the patient's perverse modes of relating to others and the specific way he related to me (Tuch, 2008). Mr. A., a married man in his early 40s, presented with idiopathic genital pain that developed shortly after he had engaged in one of a long series of casual extramarital sexual encounters. An incidental finding, which emerged only once treatment was under way, was a longstanding habit of exhibiting his penis to women, which Mr. A. made sure to let me know was "hu*mong*ous." The patient believed he exhibited himself both to distract women from noticing his "defective" body parts (he had been teased as a child for his protruding ears and sunken chest, features that made him feel "freakish," leading him to exhibit his penis as a distracting fetish) and to provide momentary relief from feeling he was nothing but a "zhlub."[2] The patient, not surprisingly, was highly narcissistic: Everything from his choice of cars to the location of his home and office was designed to impress.

Etchegoyen (1991) described the polemical (challenging) quality of perverse transferences. My patient reeked of superiority and expressed his unrelenting contempt for me. My office building, my interventions, my intellect were all "second-rate." His devaluing diatribes focused chiefly on the worthlessness of everything I was and everything I had to offer. He complained incessantly that he was not receiving the kind of eye-opening interpretations that would prove he was getting his money's worth, and he was forever challenging and goading me to finally give him something worthwhile in the way of pithy interpretations.

For months on end, Mr. A. opened each session by expressing dismay that he was continuing to see me. He figured he'd be best off cutting his losses and accepting, once and for all, that I was not the right analyst for him. He considered his inability to leave me yet another in a long list of symptoms I had yet to help him resolve—ignoring the fact his presenting genital pain had all but vanished. He reasoned I was too financially dependent on him to let him go and, if treatment were to end, I would be the one losing out, not him. Mr. A. could have picked up and left treatment months before, but he seemed to be deriving far too much sadistic pleasure watching me squirm in reaction to his unrelenting contempt as he achieved his ultimate aim: to triumph over me.

I understood Mr. A.'s transference reactions as a way of ensuring, this time around, that if anyone was going to be treated scornfully, it would be me, not him. Any countertransference urge I felt to retaliate I had to hold in check given the patient's declaration that everything I said was complete and utter "rubbish." I was cornered, in a "no win" situation with a man whose thinking conformed to a "zero-sum game" theory of human relations: There are only two roles, winners and losers, and the patient knew what he must do to stay on the right side of the ledger. Being on the receiving end of such contempt provided me with a first-hand taste of what his childhood had been like for him (the communicative aspect of projective identification). Interpretations I made along these lines went nowhere, providing further proof that indeed I was the worthless and contemptible piece of shit the patient claimed me to be and told me I was. Stanley Coen (1998, pp. 1173–1174) noted that:

> perverse defenses evoke perverse countertransferences—the opprobrium accorded perversion—in which we relish being sadistically judgmental, dominating, and attacking. The sadistic pleasure analysts take in such perverse countertransference attitudes is more difficult for us to bear than is our countertransference response of feeling excluded, alone, and insignificant when faced with narcissistic defenses ... We need to acknowledge the perverse and antagonistic affective force-field we analysts are drawn into by perverse patients who refuse to be reasonable.

Case 3: Treating a tyrannical phallic narcissist

The case of Ms. P. (Vida, 2003) illustrates how easily an analyst can lose the ability to think reflectively when treating a patient who manifests a perverse transference, though the author never identified the patient's transference as such, but her account leads readers to assume as much. Ms. P. treated her analyst in a most controlling, demeaning, and tyrannical fashion. Eventually, the analyst came to feel as if she was being held hostage. Her capacity to think gradually waned, and the best she could do was somehow endure the mistreatment until she could make her escape.

Thunder clouds were apparent early in the analysis. Ms. P. and her analyst came to loggerheads over her fee policy, which the patient found completely unacceptable. The analyst suggested that perhaps she was not the right doctor for Ms. P., which unleashed a firestorm. She writes:

I can scarily describe the firepower of her outrage at hearing this: "How dare you? What kind of analyst are you? I'm the patient. It's your job to take care of me. You're saying this is my fault. I trusted you and now you do this to me."

Ms. P. explained she had chosen this analyst to be her analyst because she knew the analyst was a self psychologist and also knew what she was needing as a patient was empathy. As it turned out, what the patient meant by empathy was the analyst's supposed obligation to unceasingly accommodate whatever Ms. P. was wanting or needing at the time. For example, when the patient found the analyst's make-up, cologne, or clothes personally offensive, she expected the analyst to change accordingly to render herself more acceptable or less offensive to the patient. "Her disruptions were of terrifying magnitude, which she insisted could only be managed by my accommodation, thus there never was a deepened understanding nor a stretching of her tolerance" (Vida, 2003, p. 29).

The patient's scorn and rage held court. She treated the analyst in the most devaluing and contemptuous manner, dismissing each of her interpretations as "trite" or "stupid." Ms. P.'s behavior proved so intimidating that the analyst "said less and less and eventually became unable to free associate or even to think during session[s]" (Vida, 2003, p. 30). I suspect what hand-cuffed the analyst, preventing her from seeing how completely unreasonable the patient was being, was her own theoretic orientation, which she admitted tended to "privilege the patient's perceptions ahead of [her] own preconceptions." (p. 29). Slowly it dawned on the analyst that "there was going to be no room for me in this analysis" (p. 28). The patient "conceived of the treatment as her being in a boat in which she held the rudder and [the analyst] the (mute) passenger" (p. 29).

Supervision proved unhelpful. What finally "broke the spell" was feedback the analyst received from the couples therapist to whom she had referred the patient and her husband. That therapist mentioned she was "appalled by the monstrous controlling presence of Ms. P." From that point forward, the analyst ceased to feel as if she was being "held hostage," writing: "For the next year and a half, I found myself regaining little by little some power of thought during Ms. P's sessions … I began to wonder if 'escape' was possible" (Vida, 2003, pp. 30–31). Ultimately, the analyst mustered up the courage to end the analysis, ten years after it had begun.

Case 4: Treating a patient with a malignant eroticized transference

One of the most challenging, dangerous, and malignant transference developments analysts face are those involving young female patients who develop an outright *eroticized* transference to a male analyst. Such patients lose their ability to keep in mind the "as if" quality of transference reactions (the analyst's reality) and become utterly convinced that their love for him is "the real deal" (indisputable reality, from the patient's perspective)—that she and her analyst were meant to be together romantically. The fact therapy brought them together, the patient argues, is an insignificant detail in the scheme of things. They might just as well have met under other circumstances, so why is the fact she is his patient of any relevance given the strength of what she is feeling? Freud (1915b) was sure such patients could not be analyzed. He referred to patients who insisted on transference gratification and turned a deaf ear to the analyst's attempt to make sense of what the patient is experiencing as those "who are accessible only to 'the logic of soup, with dumplings for arguments'" (p. 167).

It is essential we differentiate between *erotic transference* and *eroticized transference*, as Harold Blum (1973) did. An eroticized transference can be considered an extreme form of an erotic transference. Erotization, in Blum's view, is not an expression of a transference neurosis; rather, it represents a tenacious resistance that replaces what otherwise might have developed into a workable transference neurosis. Blum believed eroticized transferences develop in patients whose reality testing is impaired, whose minds are occupied by pregenital issues. Such patients form an intense, irrational, erotic preoccupation with *the person* of the analyst. The analyst likes to think of this as a transference reaction stemming from the patient's past; the analysand begs to differ, arguing it has nothing to do with the fact the patient is a patient. The erotized transference manifests in the patient's overt demand for love and sexual fulfillment from the analyst—demands that seem, to the patient, neither unreasonable nor unjustified. The patient is perennially flooded with vivid erotic fantasies involving the analyst and what their life together would be like. This is no ordinary instance of transference love; these patients more closely resemble intractable love addicts, even stalkers. The patient's conscious fear is that she will be bitterly disappointed by unrequited love, and she has no intention of letting that happen. He will be hers—there is no question about it. Transference and reality become dangerously confusing.

I supervised a candidate who had the misfortune of attempting to analyze just such a patient. Sara B. was a highly provocative woman in her late 20s married to an uneducated, unambitious, passive man a couple of decades her senior whom she agreed to marry shortly after they first met. She considered her husband sweet, kind, and loving; but she did not believe he was the type of man she wanted for a husband, and was unsure about whether she wanted to remain married. Her low self-esteem, an important presenting complaint, most likely played some role in her lacking the psychic wherewithal to leave him. Sara was an impulsive personality who tended to have an explosive temper. When she was angry with her husband, she would physically accost him, establishing an S&M quality to their way of relating to one another.

From a young age, Sara had been flirtatious—always trying to catch the eyes of older men. At the same time, she hated and distrusted men. She said of men: "They are so weak. All you have to do is flirt with them or offer them sex. It does not matter who they are. All the doctors I work with flirt with me." Sara had always had a distant relationship with her father, who "disgusted her." She had an anxious, dependent attachment to the mother. The father was considerably older than the mother, and they separated when Sara was young.

Sara idealized her analyst, who she thought to be like no man she had ever met: "I don't care that you are older than me. I know I would be happy with you. I really love you. I tell you everything. I don't share my true feelings and thoughts with anyone else." One time, after an acting-out episode in a session in which she tried to make physical contact with the analyst, the patient left a voicemail thanking him for not having taken advantage of her. "If you had given in to my wishes, I would not be able to trust any man." She seemed convinced that being with him was the path to cure—to feeling fulfilled and redeemed.

Sara came to each session dressed in a sexually provocative fashion. Given that she was coming from work, this required a "costume change" before the session began. During sessions, Sara frequently and aggressively would attempt to thrust her breasts into the analyst, playing a cat-and-mouse game with him, taking pleasure watching him squirm, loving every minute of it as he made futile, impotent attempts to keep her at arm's length. If there was a rule to break or a boundary to cross, that is precisely where you would find Sara, as if it were her *raison d'être*. She was undeterred. She did not want to be limited by the fact she was a girl; so, during latency, she cut her hair and dressed as a boy in an attempt not to be limited as to what and who she could be.

With time, Sara's behavior became impossible to manage. She would sit on the floor, inching her way toward the analyst, ready to pounce to position herself on his lap if only she could move quickly enough before he scrambled to create distance. She would position herself in ways that required he use force to maintain professional boundaries with her. She would refuse to leave the office at the end of the session. She was his last patient of the day, which played into her hand in as far as she knew the analyst did not need to attend to another patient after seeing her. She would follow him out to his car, and at one point grabbed his keys and refused to give them back, replicating an experience she had had with her father involving a television remote control. She would bombard the analyst with a flood of voicemails until he put an end to her attempts to make him available to her day and night.

The analyst attempted to interpret the infantile roots of Sara's libidinal feelings, but it fell on deaf ears. She had no interest in what he speculated to be the case regarding her love for him. What did he know? As far as she was concerned, this was how she felt—that was all there was to it. Functioning as his supervisor, I told the analyst-candidate he had best terminate the analysis because I could see no way for this treatment to become a bona fide analysis. I worried about how he was managing his counter-transference reactions, and feared he might continue to believe that, with enough interpreting, his patient would "come around" and see the light; but I had no hope that things would play out in that fashion.

Case 5: Treating a practical joker

I wrote earlier about my analysis of a young man who was referred to me by his university after he was overheard speaking about how much he relished the idea of murdering another by strangulation (Tuch, 2010). The patient, who I refer to as Corky, was excited by imagining an instance when he could see, registered in his victim's eyes, recognition that he held their life in his hands. Corky wanted not only to be *the cause* of the terror, but he also wanted literally to *be* the terror living inside the other so as to leave nothing to chance as he took complete control over his victim. Morgan (2018) notes how "the serial killer will describe in detail the sense of relief and pleasure at having total power over this victim because at the moment all the badness of impoverishment is in the victim and not in himself" (p. 197). Sometimes murder is the culmination of perverse tendencies run amok.

In Corky's case, analysis helped modulate his murderous tendencies (per a 15-year follow-up), the roots of which were discovered to lie, in part, in his experience of being mercilessly teased and taunted by schoolmates who targeted him on account of his shyness, strange quirky sense of humor, and glaring lack of social skills. Corky also reported having felt terrorized by his father's volatile temper—a man who was rarely at home, and who provided no empathy or effective guidance for his son's struggles with peers.

During the analysis, Corky described how he liked to "mess with people's minds" by casually mentioning his wish to kill. He gave me a taste of his method by comparably messing with me, which aptly illustrates how those who harbor perverse fantasies typically relate to others in a perverse fashion. During one session, early in his analysis, Corky lay down on the couch and calmly and chillingly announced: "I killed last night!" I was alarmed, caught off-guard by what he said. After allowing a few moments for his words to sink in and create their intended effect, Corky acted as if it had just then occurred to him that I might take his words literally. He apologized for having "inadvertently" shocked me, clarifying that he was referring to his having succeeded as a comedian at an open mic session the night before. So here he was introducing perverse elements into our relationship, momentarily converting the analysis into a stand-up act with me the butt of the joke. In fact, Corky knew all along what he was up to; it was all performative. He knew full well the shock his words would stir in me at first, given the nature of his presenting complaint, and he enjoyed the devilish act of setting me up and playing me in this manner. He was purposely manipulating my feelings, savoring the experience of power all the while acting as if this was the furthest thing from his mind.

Corky's humor and sadism were again on full display in another session that began with his commenting: "I failed to mention last session that your haircut made you look good ... *because it didn't.*" The way Corky delivered the line effectively set me up to expect a compliment. After teasing me, he then pulled the rug out from under that expectation, turning it into the opposite, laughing at me for having expected something good. I had been caught in the act of desiring, positioned by Corky who then exposed my naked want. Having effectively outsmarted me filled him with a sense of triumph that was expressed by an unspoken but understood declaration: Gotcha! Clearly, he was a consummate comic as well as a talented tease. His behavior is very much like that of practical jokers described by Arlow (1971), whose behavior he argued was perverse to the core.

In each of these instances, Corky pulled my leg by conducting an effective practical joke (one manifestation of perverse forms of relatedness). He indeed succeeded at getting me—and, when on stage, getting an entire audience—to be in the palm of his hand. To feel the power of making an entire room of strangers burst into uncontrollable laughter was gratifying to the extent it helped reverse his feeling of having been a vulnerable, powerless child who was the hapless victim of others. The sense of power Corky got over me and over the audience seemed to effectively substitute for the power he felt he would get from watching his victims' recognition of the power he wielded over their life as he finished them off.

This final case differs from the first four presented cases in that the patient maintained a sense of humor about how he was treating me, and seemed most interested in having me recognize his sense of humor and the clever way he manipulated my feelings. My own countertransference feelings were in league with what I sensed Corky had in mind. I was duly entertained by the way he "played" me, which lacked the sense of seriousness—even treachery—that characterized the four previous case examples.

Perverse Transference as a Method of Expressing Inner Deadness

Various factors can be thought to be at play in helping create such degrees of perversity that manifest clinically in the enactment of a perverse transference. To this list already suggested in this chapter, Ogden (1996, pp. 1122–1123) presents clinical material in support of another, wherein:

> [The perverse process] is understood as centrally involving the subversion of the recognition of the psychological death of the subject (and of the emptiness of the analytic discourse in which he or she is engaged), and the replacement of this recognition with an illusory subject, the perverse subject of analysis. The perverse subject of analysis is the narrator of the erotized, but ultimately empty drama created on the analytic

stage. The drama itself is designed to present the false impression that the narrator (the perverse subject) is alive in his or her power to excite. The perverse analytic scene and the perverse subject of analysis are jointly constructed by analyst and analysand for the purpose of evading the experience of psychological deadness and the recognition of the emptiness of the analytic discourse/intercourse.

Ogden's case is exceptional in that the other clinical examples presented in this chapter all involve male patients. One is led to believe, in the case of Judith Vida's patient, that the patient was female, but I have reason to think otherwise. This was a disguise used in the service of hiding the patient's identity—an unfortunate disguise because the case material feels different if one knows it to be an instance of how a man is treating a woman, rather than a woman treating a woman. Although the latter can still be unnerving, there is something inherent to the male–female relationship that adds a degree of danger when one is talking about male rage and a man's efforts to control women. This, then, is yet another example of toxic masculinity, a "condition" that exists at the extreme end of a continuum that constitutes the psychology of the male species. Indeed, Stoller's theories contribute meaningfully to our understanding of the psychological and emotional effects of being born male—a condition each man must come to terms with in one way or another. Unlike Freud who thought otherwise, being born male is not the ideal situation some believe it to be; and many a woman has suffered many a man whose behavior reeked of the man's desperate efforts to make peace with the psychological consequences of coming into the world male rather than female.

Notes

1 In fact, Betty Joseph (1971) used the term two years earlier.
2 A Yiddish word for someone who is generally unattractive, uninspiring, or unremarkable.

10 So What?
Providing Perspective

We begin this final chapter by considering the factors that might be further-ing the marginalization of Robert Stoller's contributions, specifically his gender theories that constitute mightily to his legacy. Many present-day gender theorists are specifically dismissive of Stoller's concept of core gender identity. These authors seem to be following in the footsteps of Jean Laplanche (2011) who declared: "When the Mahlerian [symbiosis argument] foundation col-lapses ... the whole Stollerian aetiology collapses" (p.189), which many read as meaning Laplanche negated the legitimacy of the concept of "core gender identity," which isn't precisely what he said. Even if that was Laplanche's intention, disproving Mahler doesn't disprove Stoller as we are about to see. A further matter addressed in this chapter is an impression one gets, when reading the work of present-day gender theorists, that their thinking about gender in general is heavily informed by the clinical work with patients suf-fering from gender dysphoria in particular.

The other topic highlighted in this chapter involves the extent to which Stoller's work, considered collectively, furthers our thinking about the devel-opment of male psychology. Stoller teaches us, for example, about the defen-sive function of male genital pride, which first appears during the phallic narcissistic stage of development. A persistence of phallic pride suggests a man has either regressed to, or become fixated at this stage of development, which typically manifests in behaviors, attitudes, and beliefs that are indica-tive of what is referred to colloquially "toxic masculinity." Stoller did not set out to develop a theory about male psychology, and he is not credited as having done as much; but he assuredly advanced our thinking about the consequences and challenges of being born male—his unique and very non-Freudian perspective on the matter.

In the early pages of this book, I outlined a trend to declare Stoller dead wrong when he proposed the existence of a thing he called "core gender identity." Many subsequently challenged Stoller's proto-femininity/dis-iden-tification hypothesis without seeming to realize he had proposed that hypothesis to support the notion of *gender identity* (which is about degrees of masculinity) and not core gender identity (which is more about maleness and femaleness). His proto-femininity/dis-identification hypothesis was

DOI: 10.4324/9781003609339-10

based on Margaret Mahler's (1975) proposed but subsequently disproven symbiotic phase of early childhood development. When infant observation studies (Stern 1985) established that children experience themselves as autonomous beings in the first several months of life, Mahler's symbiotic phase was widely considered to have been disproven. On that basis, the protofemininity part of Stoller's protofemininity/dis-identification hypothesis was challenged and dismissed (Axelrod, 1997; Benjamin, 1988, 1991, 1995; Christiansen, 1996; Fast, 1984; Diamond, 2004a, 2004b, 2006, 2015; Laplanche, 2011; Person Pollack, 1995, 1998). Laplanche (2011) declared: "When the Mahlerian [symbiosis argument] foundation collapses...the whole Stollerian aetiology collapses" (p. 189), but that in fact is not the case if, when referring to "aetilogy," Laplanche meant "core gender identity."

As for the dis-identification portion of Stoller's hypothesis, Micheal Diamond (2004a, 2004b, 2006, 2015) challenged Stoller's assumption that boys experience their mother's femininity as such a threat to their sense of masculinity that they feel it necessary to keep their distance lest they become feminized. If boys turn away (dis-identify) from their mothers to protect their developing sense of masculinity, Diamond argues, they only do so temporarily not permanently, as Stoller imagined.

Disproving the protofemininity/dis-identification hypothesis did not torpedo Stoller's concept of core gender identity as many had thought given that one has nothing to do with the other; the hypothesis has no bearing on core gender identity. That being what it may, many present-day gender theorists nevertheless concluded that core gender identity unquestionably had been disproven, which relieved them of the task of having to demonstrate they grasped the meaning of core gender identity and the need to debate the matter on its merits.

In fact, reading the writings of these gender theorists demonstrates the extent to which they repeatedly conflate the terms *core gender identity* and *gender identity*, which has had the untoward effect of propagating the fallacy that core gender identity is no longer a legitimate theory, when, in fact, no evidence to date has emerged that either proves or refutes the concept. Yet one continues to see this claim echoing in the writings of many of today's gender theorists, who appear certain about the stance they are taking, which aligns with what many others are repeating in an echo chamber fashion.

In fact, the argument against core gender identity is more complex. Many present-day gender theorists (Butler, 1998; Harris 2005; Saketopoulou Gozlan 2025) insist that there is no such thing as core gender identity and the thrust of their collective argument involves four related assertions: 1) Core gender identity was disproven along with the protofemininity/dis-identification hypothesis, which is clearly not the case; 2) Stoller's model of a set and fixed core gender identity is disputed by the existence of non-binary individuals for whom gender is anything but. In fact, the existence of individuals who experience their core gender identity as fluid does not logically rule out the existence of others who experience it in a very different manner, individuals who report experiencing themselves solidly and indisputably male: 3) Stoller incorrectly considered core gender identity to be innate and biologically based, a claim that represents an unfortunate misreading of Stoller's position; and 4) Gender universally is process-like and inherently unstable—neither set nor capable of ever being set. This binary, either/or assertion leaves no room for the existence of individuals who experience their core gender identity as fixed.

Saketopoulou and Pelligrini (2023) and Gozlan (2025) are adamant that there is no such thing as core gender identity, and they base their claim by noting, erroneously, that Stoller saw gender identity as chiefly biologically based. Gozlan (2025) declares gender is "No longer a core (Stoller, 1994), an internal stable sense of identity that Stoller associated with a hidden biological force…" (p. 23), echoing Saketopoulou and Pelligrini's (2023) claim: "for Stoller, core gender identity was *primarily* a 'biological force'" (pp. 17-18, italics added). The paper Saketopoulou and Pelligrini cite to back their claim (Stoller, 1964) in fact lists biological forces as *the last of the three* factors that contribute to the development of core gender identity. In his 1968 paper, Stoller reiterates the subordinate role he believes biological forces play in gender development by noting that biological forces "can *more or less modify* the effects of *the attitudes of others*" (p. 42, italics added). Laplanche (2011) himself recognized that Stoller did not prioritize biologic forces in gender development, noting: "assignment + parental attitudes…is clearly preferred by Stoller" (p. 186) in the establishment of core gender identity.

Other writers have also adopted the "no such thing" stance toward core gender identity. In her ground-breaking book Gender as Soft Assembly, a work that meaningfully advanced our thinking about the development of gender, Adrienne Harris (2005) dispenses with the concept of core gender identity in a single sentence. Judith Butler (1998) takes two of her colleagues to task for continuing to grant core gender identity standing in their writings: "Both Hansell and Elise make use of the notion of core gender identity, and it would be useful to have an explanation from them on why this metaphysically vexed notion continues to be valued" (p. 375). Butler fails to make a case of her own about why core gender identity has ceased to be a viable psychoanalytic concept and instead asks those she critiques to account for why they continue to value the concept.

Elise (1998) replied to Butler's critique in words that echo my own sentiments: "As for myself, core gender identity is a concept that I have encountered, not created, or embraced, in my attempts to penetrate the psychoanalytic corpus with my own thinking. I need to enter the body (of literature) presented to me by my forebears in order to affect that body. Otherwise, I would be having theoretical intercourse with another body of thought, and my proposed partner would remain unmoved."

Saketopoulou and Pelligrini (2023) question the existence of something that is "intrinsic to one's sense of self," (p. 17), which I read as suggesting that the "core" of Stoller's "core gender identity" refers to something that is so innate and inborn as to be unaffected by environmental factors and forces, which is not at all what Stoller had in mind. Such claims are contradicted by one of the very first things Stoller wrote about gender indicates: "we can say that the core gender identity remains unchanged throughout life; this is not to say that gender identity is not constantly developing and being modified, but only that at the core the awareness of being either a male or female remains constant" (Stoller 1964 p. 223).

Saketopoulou and Pelligrini's (2023) opine "we find the notion of core gender identity at best simplistic and at worse problematic" (p. xxii) and they challenge "the idea that *anyone* [note the absoluteness of the term used] is, at core, straight or gay or bi, cis or trans or non-binary or insert-your-gender-here" (p. xxii, italics added) on the basis that such thinking "reasserts a kind of Ptolemaic cosmology of gender and sexuality in which the true self is the centered core around which a sun of meanings rotates" (p. xii).

If I read these authors correctly, they seem to be saying that no one can seriously claim they experience themselves irrefutably male or female no matter what they say. It sounds as if they are presenting their non-binary perspective in an always/never, either/or, binary fashion—which is para-doxical. In my opinion, it cannot be the case that everyone's gender is never set and is forever in flux. The mere universality of the claim seems proble-matic. Such an assertion disregards the experience of those whose lives feel otherwise, individuals whose lived experience does not comport with what these authors claim to be universally true for one and all. Over-generalizing the experiences of non-binary individuals by applying their experiences to all human beings seems, to me, like a flaw in their reasoning.

A Laplanchian Perspective on Gender

Laplanche (2011a) insisted that gender is non-binary, writing: "Gender is plural. It is ordinarily double, as in masculine-feminine, but it is not so by nature" (p. 159). Note how Laplanche does not refer to the *male–female* binary (Stoller's concept of *core* gender identity); rather, he speaks about masculine–feminine, Stoller's concept of gender identity, which Stoller saw as non-binary to the extent most individuals experience themselves as a bit of each to varying degrees.

Laplanche sees gender, which corresponds to Stoller's concept of gender identity (degrees of masculinity/femininity), not core gender identity, as something that changes over time given the effect of *après coup*, which is thought to alter both the memory of a past event as well as its meaning. I see the matter differently. For most humans, core gender identity is lived from the start and oftentimes throughout life as a set and settled matter, which does not deny the existence of an indeterminable number of humans who do experience doubt about their gender. For such folks, core gender identity is anything but binary. The current trend to insist that gender is always, and for everyone, non-binary, in a perpetual state of becoming, unrelated to one's sense of identity, is not a model of gender many recognize as applying to their own personal lived experience.

As one grows, one's core gender identity is not likely to waiver unless conditions predispose the individual, at an early age, to develop a deeply unsettling sense of uncertainty about whether they are male or female. Otherwise, why question something that one experiences as a settled matter, something one has no problem believing in and living as one's reality, something that is causing one no problem? For those who question their core gender identity, the matter is different. Such conditions not only call for solutions of one sort or another, they also require other humans open a space within their minds to recognize and accept alterity, the reality of the essential otherness of some. We must expect and accept no less.

Laplanche's concept of après coup forms the cornerstone of the argument some present-day gender theorists make (Saketopoulou & Pellegrini, 2023; Gozlan, 2025) that gender identity is never something set in stone as Stoller's concept of core gender identity appears to claim, rather it is something that is ever evolving, in a perpetual state of becoming, in keeping with Laplanche's (2017) concept of après coup. Laplanche proposed that memories of past events are significantly and repeatedly modified over time in the process of being remembered, analogous to Freud's model of *"successive registrations"* (p. 235) and the neuroscientific concept of reconsolidation. As compelling as Laplanche's model of après coup appears to be, in fact there is no reason to think that all memories undergo the altering effects of après coup, particularly those that occur before the lifting of infantile amnesia as is the case with memories associated with the development of gender identity (around 18 months of age), which produces implicit (non-recallable) versus declarative (recallable) type memories, the latter of which seem more susceptible to après coup.

If it is true that not all memories get reworked, what conditions might favor a retrospective, après coup reconsideration of a past event? Perhaps, unresolved childhood experiences that had been troubling and unsettling at the time—enigmatic, beyond the child's capacity to fathom, as Laplanche suggests, are precisely the type of memories that trigger the après coup process. Such unsettling experiences might get psychically tagged for future reference, which sets the stage for the child to intermittently return to and reconsider the situation at later dates to solve the problem. If, despite such efforts, clarification proves allusive, it is conceivable a continuous refashioning of the original memory via après coup might be called for, which would make such instances of gender development perpetually in flux.

The evolutionary value of après coup/reconsolidation lies in its power to address select experiences, those that leave an individual in a deeply unsettled state, which requires something more happening with the experience to reach a *somewhat better* resolution. Instances when gender development runs a smoother course and arrives at a point of being a relatively settled matter, by comparison, would not seem to require the costly expenditure of psychic energy that is needed to run the après coup/reconsolidation operation (Solms 2017).

Laplanche theorized that adult caregivers send conscious and unconscious messages to the developing child that influence the child's sense of gender and contaminate his or her infantile sexuality with that of the caregiver, which had been reactivated in the process of caring for the infant. He theorized that such "enigmatic messages" must be *translated* by the child in whatever way the child does, making gender a social construct rather than something that strictly evolves intra-psychically.

Male Sexual Development: A Proposal

A sketch of the development of male psychology coalesces when several key points Stoller made about the path that leads babies to become boys who then go on to become men are considered. Unlike Freud, who saw being born male as a cakewalk, Stoller saw reasons to think otherwise. To begin with, young boys require more from their mothers than girls do to help them regulate their emotions. You might not think that to be the case given what boys grow to become—individuals who appear highly independent and self-sufficient, and proud of it—but research nevertheless establishes that boys are highly dependent on their mothers, Diamond (2015, 2021) a condition that surely continues to operate subliminally throughout a man's life, appearances to the contrary. A man's struggle with his dependency leads to a defense-driven portrayal of self-sufficiency, which can be thought to represent, in part, a reaction formation. The stereotypic model of extreme male autonomy, which helps account for why men, not women, primarily make up the pool of avoidantly attached individuals, is a ruse. No doubt, male portrayals of strength and self-sufficiency constitute noble and admirable traits, but only to the extent they don't appear clownish when overstated, as often happens in the case of toxically masculine men.

A child's dependency on his mother makes his or her efforts to separate and individuate from her more daunting for boys than it is for girls. When the boy discovers his penis, he realizes the extent to which he is other than mother both anatomically and psychically, which triggers a sense of alienation. His penis gets in the way of his ability to materially, if not spiritually, continue to identify with her. The resulting loss of a sense of closeness/likeness is emotionally devastating while, at the same time, developmentally necessary so the boy's fragile but slowly crystallizing sense of masculinity has a chance to fully blossom unimpeded by his urge for oneness with mother seeing that such a regressive urge for union is emasculating (becoming "mommy's little boy" yet again) from the standpoint of the boy's gender identity.

Dependency and vulnerability are integrally linked. A boy feels vulnerable to the potential loss of the maternal help he needs to navigate his emotional life and that persistent fear of loss persists throughout a man's life in the form of implicit (non-recallable) memories of a time when he once needed his mother to this degree. The boys sense of vulnerability also develops coincident with his discovery of his penis, which leads to the daunting realization that being male means having a lot to lose. Stoller illustrated how a young boy's burgeoning sense of masculinity is vulnerable both to instances when he is cruelly and traumatically mocked by female caregivers for proudly displaying his masculinity as well as times when boys tease other boys by challenging their sense of masculinity by calling it out.

The boy's pride in having a penis helps make up for the loss of closeness with the mother, and then some. If phallic narcissism or phallic pride gets out of hand, a boy will come to believe he is amongst a league of humans who are superior to those who are not comparably endowed. Lest we forget, penis envy was a male invention, and while the concept debatably retains a degree of legitimacy to the extent some girls feel bereft when they first realize they are lacking what other children are packing, we should not lose track of the extent to which boys cannot imagine how they would psychologically fare were they to lose their prized possession, a concern that contributes to the belief penis envy is an inevitability, which in part is a matter of projection.

Having dealt with male dependency, vulnerability, and castration anxiety, we next consider male aggression and hostility. Hormones may play a role, but there is more to the story that has to do with a man's difficulty needing a woman and his envy of women. Portrayals of male self-sufficiency are designed, in part, to defend against the underlying truth of the matter, that men not only need women but sometimes do so to such a degree that grants women power over the man. Some men over-compensate for this condition by interacting with women in an overbearing, aggressive fashion that aims to put the woman in her place, side-stepping the fear that submission will be required if the man hopes to get what it is he needs from the woman upon whom he has come to depend.

An additional source of male aggression and hostility stems from the boy's sense of feeling distanced from the mother given their anatomical differences, which stands in the way of the boy's remaining as close to her as he had once felt himself to be. Discovering the gulf that exists between them leaves the boy crestfallen; their differences can never be remedied, which generates an angry protest. The boy's alienation from the mother's body contributes to his urge to be reunited with her in the act of aggression-driven intercourse.

A third source of aggression emanates from annihilation anxiety that arises when a boy senses his wish to merge with mother, or her wish to hold him tight, threatens his sense of being an autonomous entity. This reactive aggression, which aims to obliterate the existential threat, is itself a threat to the object upon whom he has come to rely. This, in turn, generates a perverse solution that aims to retain one's bond with the object to ensure its existence and one's own ongoing existence as well. This non-hostile aggression is converted (sexualized) into sadism: "the intention to destroy [eliminate the threat to one's existence] is converted into the wish to hurt and control. In this way the object is preserved, and the viability of the relationship is ensured, albeit in sado-masochistic terms" (Glasser, 1986, p. 10).

The final piece of the puzzle regarding male psychology to be considered is the matter of psychic segregation, the need to cordon off certain impulses that typically are not permitted to enter into one's dealings with women and, instead, are sequestered in the form of fantasies and the watching of pornography, which most often run a parallel, non-intersecting course alongside a man's sexual dealings with the women in his life. Freud (1912) spelled this out in his model of the Madonna-whore complex: "Where they love [affectionately, tenderly] they do not desire [carnally—do not treat sadistically] and where they desire, they cannot love" (p. 1). Somewhat surprisingly, Freud felt this characterization applied to men *with rare exception*: "there are only a very few educated people in whom the two currents of affection and sensuality have become properly fused; the man almost always feels his respect for the woman acting as a restriction on his sexual activity, and only develops full potency when he is with a debased sexual object" (p. 185).

Stoller's thinking about male fantasy falls right in line with Freud's thinking, though he most likely would be annoyed at my noting as much given how much he opposed much of Freud's thinking about male psychology. Most often, male fantasy and pornography, on the one hand, and a man's dealings with women, on the other hand, are altogether different matters, though this is neither widely understood nor accepted. Women understandably feel excluded when confronted with the fact the man in their life has been watching porn. In fact, male fantasy and pornography entail ways for a man to selfishly save a part of himself just for himself. Such a psychic segregation not only provides a safe haven for the expression of the man's sadistic impulses, but it also represents a type of psychic retreat where men can hole up and hang out, safe from female intrusion, which can sometimes feel to men like a Trojan-horse like invasion or full-fledged occupation.

What I have just outlined is a hypothesis pieced together using components provided by Stoller's thinking. This model of male psychology is tentative and is presented in the hopes that others will enter the discourse by either presenting evidence or reasoning that refutes, supports, or hopefully, builds on what I have laid out. That is my hope. Let us see who is game to weigh in and contribute to the conversation.

References

Abraham, K. (1917). Ejaculatio praecox. In D. Bryan & A. Strachey (Trans.), *Selected papers of Karl Abraham* (pp. 64–79). Hogarth Press.

Arlow, J. (1971). Character perversion. In I. M. Marcus (Ed.), *Currents in psychoanalysis* (pp. 317–336). International Universities Press.

Axelrod, S. (1997). Developmental pathways to masculinity: A reconsideration of Greenson's "Disidentifying from mother." *Issues in Psychoanalytic Psychology, 19,* 101–115.

Bach, S. (1991). On sadomasochistic object relations. In G. Fogel & W. Myers (Eds.), *Perversions and near-perversions in clinical practice* (pp. 75–92). Yale University Press.

Balint, M. (1956). Perversions and geniality. In S. Lorand & M. Balint (Eds.), *Perversions, psychodynamics, and therapy* (pp. 16–27). Gramercy Books.

Baron-Cohen, S., Lutchmaya, S., & Knickmeyer, R. (2005). *Prenatal testosterone in mind: Amniotic fluid studies.* MIT Press/Bradford Books.

Barrett, D. (2010). *Supernormal stimuli: How primal urges overran their evolutionary purpose.* Norton.

Benjamin, J. (1988). *The bonds of love.* Pantheon.

Benjamin, J. (1990). An outline of intersubjectivity: The development of recognition. *Psychoanalytic Psychology, 7,* 33–46.

Benjamin, J. (1991). Father and daughter: Identification with difference—A contribution to gender heterodoxy. *Psychoanalytic Dialogues, 1,* 277–299.

Benjamin, J. (1995). Sameness and difference: Toward an "overinclusive" model of gender development. *Psychoanalytic Inquiry, 15,* 125–142.

Bion, W. R. (1962). *Learning from experience.* Heinemann.

Bloom, H. (1994). *The western canon:The books and school of the ages.* Harcourt Brace.

Blum, H. (1973). The concept of erotized transference. *Journal of the American Psychoanalytic Association, 21,* 61–76.

Boies, S., Cooper, A., & Osborne, C. (2004). Variations in internet-related problems and psychosocial functioning in online sexual activities: Implications for social and sexual development of young adults. *Cyberpsychology and Behavior, 7,* 207–230.

Butler, J. (1998). Analysis to the Core: Commentary on Papers by James H. Hansell and Dianne Elise. *Psychoanalytic Dialogues, 8,* 373–377.

Carnes, P., Delmonico, D., & Griffin, E. (2001). *In the shadows of the net: Breaking free from compulsive online sexual behaviour.* Hazelden.

Cavell, S. (1988). Two cheers for romance. In W. Gaylin & E. Person (Eds.), *Passionate attachments: Thinking about love* (pp. 85–99). The Free Press.

Chasseguet-Smirgel, J. (1976). Freud and female sexuality. *International Journal of Psychoanalysis*, 57, 275–287.

Chasseguet-Smirgel, J. (1981). Loss of reality in perversions: With special reference to fetishism. *Journal of the American Psychoanalytic Association*, 29, 511–534.

Chasseguet-Smirgel, J. (1985). *Creativity and perversion*. Free Association Books.

Chasseguet-Smirgel, J. (1991). Sadomasochism in the perversions: Some thoughts on the destruction of reality. *Journal of the American Psychoanalytic Association*, 39, 399–415.

Christiansen, A. (1996). Masculinity and its vicissitudes: Reflections on some gaps in the psychoanalytic theory of male identity formation. *Psychoanalytic Review*, 83, 97–124.

Christoffel, H. (1936). Exhibitionism and exhibitionists. *International Journal of Psychoanalysis*, 17, 321–345.

Coen, S. (1981). Sexualization as a predominant mode of defense. *Journal of the American Psychoanalytic Association*, 29, 893–920.

Coen, S. (1998). Perverse defenses in neurotic patients. *Journal of the American Psychoanalytic Association*, 46, 1169–1194.

Connell, R. (1987). *Gender and Power: Society, the Person and Sexual Politics*. Stanford University Press.

Cooper, A. (1991). The unconscious core of perversion. In G. Fogel & W. Myers (Eds.), *Perversions and near-perversions in clinical practice* (pp. 17–35). Yale University Press.

Cooper, A. (1998). Sexuality and the internet: Surfing into the new millennium. *Cyberpsychology and Behavior*, 1, 181–187.

Cooper, A., Delmonico, D., Griffin-Shelley, E., & Mathy, R. (2004a). Online sexual activity: An examination of potentially problematic behaviors. *Sexual Addiction and Compulsivity*, 11, 129–143.

Cooper, A., Galbreath, N., & Becker, M. (2004b). Sex on the internet: Furthering our understanding of men with online sexual problems. *Psychology of Addictive Behaviors*, 18, 223–230.

Cooper, A., Putnam, D., Planchon, L., & Boies, S. (1999). Online sexual compulsivity: Getting tangled in the net. *Sexual Addiction and Compulsivity*, 6, 79–104.

Corbett, K. (2008). Gender Now. *Psychoanalytic Dialogues*, 18, 838–856.

Corbett, K., Dimen, M., Goldner, V., & Harris, A. (2014). Talking sex, talking gender: A roundtable. *Studies in Gender and Sexuality*, 15, 295–317.

Corrigan, E. G., & Gordon, P.-E. (1995). The mind as an object. In E. G. Corrigan & P.-E. Gordon (Eds.), *The mind object: Precocity and pathology of self-sufficiency* (pp. 1–21). Jason Aronson.

Critelli, J., & Bivona, J. (2008). Women's erotic rape fantasies: An evaluation of theory and research. *Journal of Sex Research*, 45, 57–70.

Davies, J., & Frawley, M. (1994). *Treating the adult survivor of childhood sexual abuse: A psychoanalytic perspective*. Basic Books.

De Masi, F. (1999). *The sadomasochistic perversion: The entity and the theories*. Karnac.

de Sade, Marquis (1966). *The 120 days of Sodom and other writings*. Random House.

de Vries, A. L. C., Noens, I. L. J., Cohen-Kettenis, P. T., van Berckelaer-Onnes, I. A., & Doreleijers, T. A. (2010). *Autism spectrum disorders in gender dysphoric children and adolescents. Journal of Autism and Developmental Disorders*, 40(8), 930–936.

DeCarlo, T. (2004, May). A fresh look at Diane Arbus. *Smithsonian Magazine*. Retrieved from https://www.smithsonianmag.com/arts-culture/a-fresh-look-at-diane-arbus-99861134/, December 13, 2017.

Delmonico, D. (2002). Sex on the superhighway. In P. J. Carnes & K. E. Adams (Eds.), *Clinical management of sex addiction* (pp. 239–254). Routledge.

Delmonico, D., & Griffin, E. (2008). Cybersex and the E-teen: What marriage and family therapists should know. *Journal of Marital and Family Therapy*, 34, 431–444.

Diamond, M. (2004a). Accessing the multitude within: A psychoanalytic perspective on the transformation of masculinity at mid-life. *International Journal of Psychoanalysis*, 85, 45–64.

Diamond, M. (2004b). The shaping of masculinity: Revisioning boys turning away from their mothers to construct male gender identity. *International Journal of Psychoanalysis*, 85, 359–380.

Diamond, M. (2006). Masculinity unraveled: The roots of male gender identity and the shifting of male ego ideals throughout life. *Journal of the American Psychoanalytic Association*, 54, 1099–1130.

Diamond, M. (2015). The elusiveness of masculinity: Primordial vulnerability, lack, and the challenges of male development. *Psychoanalytic Quarterly*, 84, 47–102.

Diamond, M. (2021). *Masculinity and its discontents: The male psyche and the inherent tensions of maturing manhood*. Routledge.

Drury, S. S., Theall, K., Gleason, M. M., Smyke, A. T., De Vivo, I., Wong, J. Y. Y., Fox, N. A., Zeanah, C. H., & Nelson, C. A. (2012). Telomere length and early severe social deprivation: Linking early adversity and cellular aging. *Molecular Psychiatry*, 17, 719–772.

Elise, D. (1998a). Gender Repertoire: Body, Mind, and Bisexuality. *Psychoanalytic Dialogues*, 8, 353–371.

Elise, D. (1998b). Penetrating Psychoanalytic Theory: Reply to Commentary. *Psychoanalytic Dialogues*, 8, 383–384.

Etchegoyen, H. (1978). Some thoughts on transference perversion. *International Journal of Psychoanalysis*, 59, 45–53.

Etchegoyen, H. (1991). *The fundamentals of psychoanalytic technique*. Karnac.

Fairbairn, W. D. (1952). *Psychoanalytic studies of the personality*. Tavistock.

Fast, I. (1984). *Gender identity*. Analytic Press.

Ferenczi, S. (1933). A confusion of tongues (J. Dupont, Trans.). *International Journal of Psychoanalysis*, 30, 225–235.

Figlio, K. (2010). Phallic and seminal masculinity: A theoretical and clinical confusion. *International Journal of Psychoanalysis*, 91, 119–139.

Filippini, S. (2005). Perverse relationships: The perspective of the perpetrator. *International Journal of Psychoanalysis*, 86, 755–773.

Fink, B. (2016). *Lacan on love: An exploration of Lacan's Seminar VIII: Transference*. Routledge.

Fisher, D. J. (1996). Remembering Robert J. Stoller (1924–1991). *Psychoanalytic Review*, 83, 1–9.

Freud, S. (1905). Three essays on the theory of sexuality. In J. Strachey (Ed. & Trans.), *The standard edition of the complete psychological works of Sigmund Freud* (Vol. 7, pp. 123–246). Hogarth Press.

Freud, S. (1910). Five lectures on psycho-analysis. In J. Strachey (Ed. & Trans.), *The standard edition of the complete psychological works of Sigmund Freud* (Vol. 11, pp. 1–56). Hogarth Press.

Freud, S. (1912). On the universal tendency to debasement in the sphere of love. In J. Strachey (Ed. & Trans.), *The standard edition of the complete psychological works of Sigmund Freud* (Vol. 11, pp. 179–190). Hogarth Press.

Freud, S. (1915a). Instincts and their vicissitudes. In J. Strachey (Ed. & Trans.), *The standard edition of the complete psychological works of Sigmund Freud* (Vol. 14, pp. 109–140). Hogarth Press.

Freud, S. (1915b). Observations on transference-love (Further recommendations on the technique of psychoanalysis III). In J. Strachey (Ed. & Trans.), *The standard edition of the complete psychological works of Sigmund Freud* (Vol. 12, pp. 127–171). Hogarth Press.

Freud, S. (1924). The dissolution of the Oedipus complex. In J. Strachey (Ed. & Trans.), *The standard edition of the complete psychological works of Sigmund Freud* (Vol. 19, pp. 173–179). Hogarth Press.

Freud, S. (1925). Negation. In J. Strachey (Ed. & Trans.), *The standard edition of the complete psychological works of Sigmund Freud* (Vol. 19, pp. 233–240). Hogarth Press.

Freud, S. (1927). Fetishism. In J. Strachey (Ed. & Trans.), *The standard edition of the complete psychological works of Sigmund Freud* (Vol. 21, pp. 147–158). Hogarth Press.

Freud, S. (1931). Female sexuality. In J. Strachey (Ed. & Trans.), *The standard edition of the complete psychological works of Sigmund Freud* (Vol. 21, pp. 221–244). Hogarth Press.

Freud, S. (1933). New introductory lectures on psycho-analysis. Lecture XXXIII: Femininity. In J. Strachey (Ed. & Trans.), *The standard edition of the complete psychological works of Sigmund Freud* (Vol. 22, pp. 1–182). Hogarth Press.

Freud, S. (1938). Splitting of the ego in the process of defence. In J. Strachey (Ed. & Trans.), *The standard edition of the complete psychological works of Sigmund Freud* (Vol. 23, pp. 271–278). Hogarth Press.

Friedman, R., & Downey, J. (2008). Sexual differentiation of behavior: The foundation of a developmental model of psychosexuality. *Journal of the American Psychoanalytic Association*, 56, 147–175.

Galenson, E., & Roiphe, H. (1976). Some suggested revisions concerning early female development. *Journal of the American Psychoanalytic Association*, 24, 29–57.

Galenson, E. (1988). Presentations of Gender: By Robert J. Stoller. New Haven, Conn.: Yale Univ. Press, 1985, 219 pp., $22.00. *Journal of the American Psychoanalytic Association*, 36, 1075–1079.

Gay, P. (1988). *Freud: A life for our time*. Norton.

Gebhard, P., Gagnon, J., Pomeroy, W., & Christenson, C. V. (1965). *Sex offenders: An analysis of types*. Harper & Row.

Gedo, J. E. (1988). Review, Observing the Erotic Imagination: By Robert J. Stoller. New Haven: Yale Univ. Press, 1985, xi & 228 pp. *Journal of the American Psychoanalytic Association*, 36, 529–532.

Ghent, E. (1990). Masochism, submission, surrender: Masochism as a perversion of surrender. *Contemporary Psychoanalysis*, 26, 108–136.

Gil, H. (1987). Effects of Oedipal triumph caused by collapse or death of the parent. *International Journal of Psychoanalysis*, 68, 251–260.

Gittleson, H., Eacott, S., & Mehta, B. (1978). Victims of indecent exposure. *British Journal of Psychiatry*, 132, 61–66.

Glasser, M. (1979). Some aspects of the role of aggression in the perversions. In I. Rosen (Ed.), *Sexual deviation* (2nd ed.) (pp. 278–305). Oxford University Press.

Glasser, M. (1985). The "weak spot": Some observations on male sexuality. *International Journal of Psychoanalysis*, 66, 405–414.

Glasser, M. (1986). Identification and its vicissitudes as observed in the perversions. *International Journal of Psychoanalysis*, 67, 9–16.

Glasser, M. (1992). Problems in the psychoanalysis of certain narcissistic disorders. *International Journal of Psychoanalysis*, 73, 493–503.

Glasser, M. (2003). Aggression and sadism in the perversions. In I. Rosen (Ed.), *Sexual deviation* (3rd ed.) (pp. 279–299). Oxford University Press.

Glover, E. (1933). The relation of perversion-formation to the development of reality-sense. *International Journal of Psychoanalysis*, 14, 486–504.

Goldberg, A. (1995). *The problem of perversion: A view from self-psychology*. Yale University Press.

Goodman, A. (1993). The addictive process: A psychoanalytic understanding. *Journal of the American Academy of Psychoanalysis*, 21, 89–105.

Gozlan, O. (2025). Novel revolts as crafting a self. *Psychoanalytic Quarterly*, 94(1), 5–27.

Green, A. (2001). *The chains of Eros: The sexual in psychoanalysis*. Karnac.

Greenacre, P. (1960). Further notes on fetishism. *Psychoanalytic Study of the Child*, 15, 191–207.

Greenacre, P. (2003). Fetishism. In I. Rosen (Ed.), *Sexual deviation* (3rd ed.) (pp. 88–110). Oxford University Press.

Greenson, R. (1966). A transvestite boy and a hypothesis. *International Journal of Psychoanalysis*, 47, 396–403.

Greenson, R. (1968). Dis-identifying from mother: Its special importance for the boy. *International Journal of Psychoanalysis*, 49, 370–374.

Grossman, L. (1992). An example of "character perversion" in a woman. *Psychoanalytic Quarterly*, 61, 581–589.

Grossman, L. (1993). The perverse attitude toward reality. *Psychoanalytic Quarterly*, 62, 422–436.

Grossman, L. (1996). Psychic reality and perversions. *International Journal of Psychoanalysis*, 77, 1233–1234.

Halberstadt-Freud, H. C. (1991). *Freud, Proust, perversion, and love*. Swets and Zeitlinger.

Harper, C., & Hodgins, D. (2016). Examining correlates of problematic internet pornography use among university students. *Journal of Behavioral Addictions*, 5, 179–191.

Harris, A. (2005). *Gender as soft assembly*. Hillsdale, NJ: Analytic Press.

Herdt, G. (2020). Robert J. Stoller in the clinic and the village. *Psychoanalysis and History*, 22, 15–33.

Herdt, G. & Stoller, R. J. (1990). *Intimate communications: Erotics and the study of culture*. Columbia University Press.

Herzog, J. (2001). *Father hunger: Explorations with adults and children*. Analytic Press.

Herzog, J. (2004). Father hunger and narcissistic deformation. *Psychoanalytic Quarterly*, 73, 893–914.

Hilton, D. L. (2013). Pornography addiction: A supranormal stimulus considered in the context of neuroplasticity. *Socioaffective Neuroscience and Psychology*, 3, https://pmc.ncbi.nlm.nih.gov/articles/PMC3960020/.

Horney, K. (1932). Observation on a specific difference in the dread felt by men and by women respectively for the opposite sex. *International Journal of Psychoanalysis*, 13, 348–360.

Horney, K. (1936). The problem of the negative therapeutic reaction. *Psychoanalytic Quarterly*, 5, 29–44.

Jimenez, J. (2004). A psychoanalytic phenomenology of perversion. *International Journal of Psychoanalysis*, 85, 65–82.

Jong, E. (1973). *Fear of Flying*. New York: Random House.

Joseph, B. (1971). A clinical contribution to the analysis of a perversion. *International Journal of Psychoanalysis*, 52, 441–449.

Kafka, M. (2010). Hypersexual disorder: A proposed diagnosis for DSM-V. *Archives of Sexual Behavior*, 39, 377–400.

Kallitsounaki, A., & Williams, D. M. (2022a). Implicit and explicit gender-related cognition, gender dysphoria, autistic-like traits, and mentalizing: Differences between autistic and non-autistic cisgender and transgender adults. *Archives of Sexual Behavior*, 51(7), 3583–3600.

Kallitsounaki, A., & Williams, D. M. (2022b). Autism spectrum disorder and gender dysphoria/incongruence: A systematic literature review and meta-analysis. *Journal of Autism and Developmental Disorders*, 53(8), 3103–3117.

Kanin, E. (1982). Female rape fantasies: A victimization study. *Victimology*, 7, 114–121.

Kernberg, O. F. (1991). Aggression and love in the relationship of the couple. *Journal of the American Psychoanalytic Association*, 39, 45–70.

Kernberg, O. F. (1992). *Aggression in personality disorders and perversions*. Yale University Press.

Kernberg, O. F. (2011). The sexual couple: A psychoanalytic exploration. *Psychoanalytic Review*, 98, 217–245.

Khan, M. (1979). *Alienation in perversions*. International Universities Press.

Kirshner, L. (2005). Rethinking desire: The *objet petit a* in Lacanian theory. *Journal of the American Psychoanalytic Association*, 53, 83–102.

Kochanska, G., Coy, K. C., & Murray, K. T. (2001). The development of self-regulation in the first four years of life. *Child Development*, 72, 1091–1111.

Lacan, J. (2015). *The seminar of Jacques Lacan, Book VIII: Transference* (1960–1961) (J.-A. Miller, Ed., & B. Fink, Trans.). Polity.

Landis, J. (1956). Experiences of 500 children with adult sexual deviation. *Psychiatric Quarterly*, 30(Suppl), 91–109.

Laplanche, J. (1989). *New foundations for psychoanalysis* (D. Macey, Trans.). Blackwell.

Laplanche, J. (1997). The theory of seduction and the problem of the other. *International Journal of Psychoanalysis*, 78, 653–666.

Laplanche, J. (2011a). Gender, sex and the *sexual*. In J. Fletcher (Ed.); J. Fletcher, J. House, & N. Ray (Trans.), *Freud and the sexual: Essays 2000–2006* (pp. 159–202). International Psychoanalytic Books.

Laplanche, J. (2011b). Starting from the fundamental anthropological situation. In J. Fletcher (Ed.); J. Fletcher, J. House, & N. Ray (Trans.), *Freud and the sexual: Essays 2000–2006* (pp. 99–113). International Psychoanalytic Books.

Lasky, R. (1984). Dynamics and problems in the treatment of the "Oedipal winner." *Psychoanalytic Review*, 71, 351–374.

Laufer, M. (1976). The central masturbation fantasy, the final sexual organization, and adolescence. *Psychoanalytic Study of the Child*, 31, 297–316.

Laufer, M. (1981). The psychoanalyst and the adolescent's sexual development. *Psychoanalytic Study of the Child*, 36, 181–189.

Laufer, M. (1989). Adolescent sexuality: A body/mind continuum. *Psychoanalytic Study of the Child*, 44, 281–294.

Lawrence, D. H. (1913). *Sons and lovers*. Duckworth.

Lawrence, D. H. (1915). *The rainbow*. Methuen.

Lawrence, D. H. (1920). *Women in love*. Vintage.

Lawrence, D. H. (1922). Parent love. In *Fantasia of the unconscious* (pp. 165–185). Thomas Seltzer.

Lawrence, D. H. (1923). *The captain's doll*. Thomas Seltzer.

Lawrence, F. (1935/1983). *Not I, but the wind*. Granada.

Lihn, H. (1970). Fetishism: A case report. *International Journal of Psychoanalysis*, 51, 351–358.

Lihn, H. (1971). Sexual masochism: A case report. *International Journal of Psychoanalysis*, 52, 469–478.

Macdonald, J. (1973). *Indecent exposure*. Charles C. Thomas.

Mahler, M. (1975). Discussion of "Healthy parental influences on the earliest development of masculinity in baby boys," by R. Stoller. In J. Lindon (Ed.), *Psychoanalytic forum* (Vol. 5). International Universities Press.

Mahler, M., Pine, F., & Bergman, A. (1975). *The psychological birth of the human infant*. Basic Books.

Malcolm, R. (1970). The mirror: A perverse sexual phantasy in a woman seen as a defense against a psychotic breakdown. In E. B. Spillius (Ed.), *Melanie Klein today* (Vol. 2, pp. 115–137. Routledge.

Martel, M. M., Klump, K., Nigg, J. T., Breedlove, S. M., & Sisk, C. L. (2009). Potential hormonal mechanisms of attention-deficit/hyperactivity disorder and major depressive disorder: A new perspective. *Hormones and Behavior*, 55, 465–479.

McDougall, J. (1995). *The many faces of Eros: A psychoanalytic exploration of human sexuality*. Norton.

Meltzer, D. (1973). *Sexual states of mind*. Clunie.

Money, J. (1973). *Man and woman, boy and girl: Differentiation and dimorphism of gender identity from conception to maturity*. Johns Hopkins University Press.

Money, J., Hampson, J. G., & Hampson, J. L. (1955a). An examination of some basic sexual concepts: The evidence of human hermaphroditism. *Bulletin of Johns Hopkins Hospital*, 97, 301–310.

Money, J., Hampson, J. G., & Hampson, J. L. (1955b). Hermaphroditism: Recommendations concerning assignment of sex, change of sex, and psychologic management. *Bulletin of Johns Hopkins Hospital*, 97, 284–300.

Money, J., Hampson, J. G. & Hampson, J. L. (1957). Imprinting and the establishment of gender role. *Archives of Neurology and Psychiatry, 77,* 333–336.

Moore, H. (1962). *The collected letters of D. H. Lawrence* (Vol. 1). Viking.

Morgan, D. (2018). Perverse patients' use of the body—their own and that of others. In D. Morgan & S. Ruszczynski (Eds.), *The Portman papers: Lectures on violence, perversion, and delinquency* (pp. 193–202). Routledge.

Morgan, D., & Ruszczynski, S. (Eds.). (2018). *The Portman papers: Lectures on violence, perversion, and delinquency.* Routledge.

Morton, A. (1999). *Monica's story.* St. Martin's Press.

Odlaug, B., Lust, K., Schreiber, L., Christenson, G., Derbyshire, K., Harvanko, A., et al. (2013). Compulsive sexual behavior in young adults. *Annals of Clinical Psychiatry, 25,* 193–200.

Ogden, T. (1996). The perverse subject of analysis. *Journal of the American Psychoanalytic Association, 44,* 1121–1146.

Parsons, M. (2000). Sexuality and perversion a hundred years on: Discovering what Freud discovered. *International Journal of Psychoanalysis, 81,* 37–49.

Paul, P. (2005). *Pornified: How pornography is transforming our lives, our relationships, and our families.* Times Books.

Pauley, D. (2018). The negative transitional object: Theoretical elaboration and clinical illustration. *Psychoanalytic Dialogues, 28,* 131–143.

Pelletier, L., & Herold, E. (1988). The relationship of age, sex guilt, and sexual experience with female sexual fantasies. *Journal of Sex Research, 24,* 250–256.

Person, E., & Ovesey, L. (1983). Psychoanalytic theories of gender identity. *Journal of the America Academy of Psychoanalysis, 11,* 203–226.

Pollack, W. (1995). Deconstructing dis-identification: Rethinking psychoanalytic concepts of male development. *Psychoanalytic Psychotherapy, 12,* 30–45.

Pollack, W. (1998). *Real boys: Rescuing our sons from the myths of boyhood.* Random House.

Privara, M., & Bob, P. (2023). Pornography consumption and cognitive-affective distress. *Journal of Nervous and Mental Disease, 211,* 641–646.

Rey, J. H. (1979). Schizoid phenomena in the borderline patient. In J. Leboit & A. Capponi (Eds.), *Advances in psychotherapy of the borderline patient.* Jason Aronson.

Rey, J. H. (1994). *Universals of psychoanalysis in the treatment of psychotic and borderline states.* Free Association Books.

Riesenberg-Malcolm, R. (1992). As-if: The experience of not learning. In R. Anderson (Ed.), *Clinical lectures on Klein and Bion* (pp. 114–124). Routledge.

Rosenfeld, H. (1987). Destructive narcissism and the death instinct. In *Impasse and interpretation: Therapeutic and anti-therapeutic factors in the psychoanalytic treatment of psychotic, borderline, and neurotic patients* (pp. 105–132). Routledge.

Ross, M., Månsson, S.-A., & Daneback, K. (2012). Prevalence, severity, and correlates of problematic sexual internet use in Swedish men and women. *Archives of Sexual Behavior, 41,* 459–466.

Rubin, M. (2025). Calamities and secrets, the power of the fetish. *Psychoanalytic Dialogues, 35*(2), 106–120.

Ruszczynski, S. (2018). The problem of certain psychic realities: Aggression and violence as perverse solution. In D. Morgan & S. Ruszczynski (Eds.), *Lectures on violence, perversion, and delinquency* (pp. 23–41). Routledge.

Sachs, H. (1942). A review of Reik's masochism in modern man. *Psychoanalytic Quarterly*, 11, 555–561.

Saketopoulou, A., & Pellegrini, A. (2023). *Gender without identity*. The Unconscious in Translation.

Sánchez-Medina, A. (2002). Perverse thought. *International Journal of Psychoanalysis*, 83, 1345–1359.

Siegman, A. (1964). Exhibitionism and fascination. *Journal of the American Psychoanalytic Association*, 12, 315–335.

Silverman, D. (1941). The treatment of exhibitionism: An experience in cooperation between police and psychiatric clinic. *Bulletin of the Menninger Clinic*, 5, 85–93.

Snaith, R. (1983). Exhibitionism: A clinical conundrum. *British Journal of Psychiatry*, 143, 231–235.

Socarides, C. (1988). *The preoedipal origin and psychoanalytic therapy of sexual perversions*. International Universities Press.

Sperling, M. (1947). The analysis of an exhibitionist. *International Journal of Psychoanalysis*, 28, 32–45.

Stein, R. (2005). Why perversion? "False love" and the perverse pact. *International Journal of Psychoanalysis*, 86, 775–799.

Steiner, J. (1993). *Psychic retreats: Pathological organizations in psychotic, neurotic, and borderline patients*. Routledge.

Stekel, W. (1952). *Patterns of psychosexual infantilism* (E. A. Gutheil, Ed.). Liveright.

Stern, D. (1985). *The interpersonal world of the infant: A view from psychoanalysis and developmental psychology*. Basic Books.

Stoller, R. J. (1964). A contribution to the study of gender identity. *International Journal of Psychoanalysis*, 45, 220–226.

Stoller, R. J. (1965). The sense of maleness. *Psychoanalytic Quarterly*, 34, 207–218.

Stoller, R. J. (1968). *Sex and gender*. Science House.

Stoller, R. J. (1973). The male transsexual as "experiment". *International Journal of Psychoanalysis*, 54, 215–225.

Stoller, R. J. (1974a). The creation of illusion: Extreme femininity in boys. *Annual of Psychoanalysis*, 2, 197–212.

Stoller, R. J. (1974b). Hostility and mystery in perversion. *International Journal of Psychoanalysis*, 55, 425–434.

Stoller, R. J. (1975). *Perversion: The erotic form of hatred*. Pantheon.

Stoller, R. J. (1976a). Primary femininity. *Journal of the American Psychoanalytic Association*, 24, 59–78.

Stoller, R. J. (1976b). *Sex and gender, Vol. II: The transsexual experiment*. Jason Aronson.

Stoller, R. J. (1979). A contribution to the study of gender identity: Follow-up. *International Journal of Psychoanalysis*, 60, 433–441.

Stoller, R. J. (1985a). *Presentations of gender*. Yale University Press.

Stoller, R. J. (1985b). *Observing the erotic imagination*. Yale University Press.

Stoller, R. J. (1991). The term perversion. In G. Fogel & W. Myers (Eds.), *Perversions and near-perversions in clinical practice* (pp. 36–56). Yale University Press.

Stoller, R. J. (1993). *Porn: Myths for the twentieth century*. Yale University Press.

Stoller, R. J. (2009). *Sweet dreams, erotic plots: A previously unpublished work by Robert Stoller*. Karnac.

Stoller, R. J., & Herdt, G. H. (1982). The development of masculinity: A cross-cultural contribution. *Journal of the American Psychoanalytic Association*, 30, 29–59.

Stoller, R. J., & Levine, I. S. (1993). *Coming attractions: The making of an X-rated movie*. Yale University Press.

Stoller, R. J., & Wagonfeld, S. (1982). Gender and gender role. *Journal of the American Psychoanalytic Association*, 30, 185–196.

Stoller, R. J., Marmor, J., Bieber, I., Gold, R., Socarides, C., Green, R., and Spitzer, R. (1973). A symposium: Should homosexuality be in the APA nomenclature? *American Journal of Psychiatry*, 130(11), 1207–1216.

Strassberg, D., & Lockerd, L. (1998). Force in women's sexual fantasies. *Archives of Sexual Behavior*, 27, 403–414.

Sussman, S. (2007). Sexual addiction among teens: A review. *Sexual Addiction and Compulsivity*, 14, 257–278.

Sweet, A. (2014). Objects of desire and the mediated self: Addictions, compulsions, and fetishism in the technoculture arena. *Psychoanalytic Psychotherapy*, 28, 176–192.

Tausk, V. (1951). On masturbation. *Psychoanalytic Study of the Child*, 6, 61–79.

Terr, L. (1979). Children of Chowchilla: A study of psychic trauma. *Psychoanalytic Study of the Child*, 34, 547–623.

Tinbergen, N. (1989). *The study of instinct*. Clarendon.

Toates, F. (2014). *How sexual desire works: The enigmatic urge*. Cambridge University Press.

Toronto, E. (2009). Time out of mind: Dissociation in the virtual world. *Psychoanalytic Psychology*, 26, 117–133.

Tronick, E. Z., & Weinberg, M. K. (2000). Gender differences and their relation to maternal depression. In S. L. Johnson, T. M. Field, N. Schneiderman, & P. M. McCabe (Eds.), *Stress, coping, and depression* (pp. 23–34). Lawrence Erlbaum Associates.

Tuch, R. (2000). *The single woman-married man syndrome*. Rowman & Littlefield.

Tuch, R. (2010). Murder on the mind: Tyrannical power and other points along the perverse spectrum. *International Journal of Psychoanalysis*, 91, 141–162.

Tuch, R. H. (1999). The construction, reconstruction, and deconstruction of memory in the light of social cognition. *Journal of the American Psychoanalytic Association*, 47, 153–186.

Tuch, R. H. (2008). Unravelling the riddle of exhibitionism: A lesson in the power tactics of perverse interpersonal relationships. *International Journal of Psychoanalysis*, 89, 143–160.

van der Aa, N., Overbeek, G., Engels, R., Scholte, R., Meerkerk, G.-J., & Van den Eijnden, R. (2009). Daily and compulsive internet use and well-being in adolescence: A diathesis-stress model based on big five personality traits. *Journal of Youth and Adolescence*, 38, 765–776.

Vida, J. (2003). The indispensable "difficult event". In J. Reppen & M. A. Shulman (Eds.), *Failures in psychoanalytic treatment* (pp. 17–36). International Universities Press.

Waelder, R. (2007). The principle of multiple function: Observations on over-determination. *Psychoanalytic Quarterly*, 76, 75–92.

Warrier, V., Greenberg, D. M., Weir, E., Buckingham, C., Smith, P., Lai, M.-C., Allison, C., & Baron-Cohen, S. (2020). Elevated rates of autism, other neurodevelopmental and psychiatric diagnoses, and autistic traits in transgender and gender-diverse individuals. *Nature Communications*, 11 (1), 3959.

Weinberg, M. K., Olson, K. L., Beeghly, M., & Tronick, E. Z. (2006). Making up is hard to do, especially for mothers with high levels of depressive symptoms and their infant sons. *Journal of Child Psychology and Psychiatry*, 47, 670–683.

Winnicott, D. W. (1971). *Playing and reality*. Basic Books.

Wood, H. (2011). The internet and its role in the escalation of sexually compulsive behaviour. *Psychoanalytic Psychotherapy*, 25, 127–142.

Wood, H. (2013). The nature of the addiction in "sex addiction" and paraphilias. In M. Bower, R. Hale, & H. Wood (Eds.), *Addictive states of mind* (pp. 151–174). Karnac.

Wood, H. (2014). Working with problems of perversion. *British Journal of Psychotherapy*, 30, 422–437.

Woods, J. (2013). Group analytic therapy for compulsive users of internet pornography. *Psychoanalytic Psychotherapy*, 27, 306–318.

Wurmser, L. (1993). *The riddle of masochism and the addiction to suffering*. Springer.

Wurmser, L. (2007). *Torment me, but don't abandon me: Psychoanalysis of the severe neuroses in a new key*. Rowman & Littlefield.

Young, K. (1999). The evaluation and treatment of internet addiction. In L. Vande-Creek & T. Jackson (Eds.), *Innovations in clinical practice: A source book* (pp. 19–31). Professional Resource Press.

Young, K. (2007). Cognitive behavior therapy with internet addicts: Treatment outcomes and implications. *Cyberpsychology and Behavior*, 1, 181–187.

Zeanah, C., Egger, H., Smyke, A., Nelson, C., Fox, N., Marshal, P., & Gutherie, D. (2009). Institutional rearing and psychiatric disorders in Romanian preschool children. *American Journal of Psychiatry*, 166, 777–785.

Zimmer, R. (2003). Perverse modes of thought. *Psychoanalytic Quarterly*, 72, 905–938.

Index

For Product Safety Concerns and Information please contact our EU
representative GPSR@taylorandfrancis.com
Taylor & Francis Verlag GmbH, Kaufingerstraße 24, 80331 München, Germany